ADVANCES
IN
CHINESE
COMPUTER SCIENCE

Volume 2

T0324879

ADVANCES IN CHINESE COMPUTER SCIENCE

Volume 2

edited by
Xu Kongshi
Institute of Software
Academia Sinica
Beijing

World Scientific
Singapore • New Jersey • London • Hong Kong

Published by

World Scientific Publishing Co. Pte. Ltd.,
P O Box 128, Farrer Road, Singapore 9128
USA office: 687 Hartwell Street, Teaneck, NJ 07666
UK office: 73 Lynton Mead, Totteridge, London N20 8DH

ADVANCES IN CHINESE COMPUTER SCIENCE — Vol. 2

ISBN 9971-50-791-9

Printed in Singapore by JBW Printers & Binders Pte. Ltd.

CONTENTS

ADVANCES IN CHINESE COMPUTER SCIENCE

Volume 2

RES:PCB ROUTING DESIGN EXPERT SYSTEM

He Chenwu & Chen Min
East-China Research Institute of Computer Technology

Abstract

This paper describes a new PCB routing system based on AI techniques. In order to raise the routing completion rates, RES adopts a knowledge-based method. It incorporates the designer's knowledge as a set of rules.

To develop a knowledge-based routing system which can solve a large scale real problem, we adopted a hybrid approach by combining the PROLOG and PASCAL language. Further, we proposed a new event-driven inference engine and a knowledge representation method.

1. Introduction

A routing problem in PCB layout design is determining an appropriate connecting path. The path must meet all physical constraints for each given net. From a computational point of view, a routing problem is considered to be a hard combinatorial problem. Further, it is obviously a large-scale problem. Routing is the most time consuming phase in the entire designing process. It is far too difficult to complete the whole design by only using automatic programs with deterministic algorithms. The total designing process consists of both automatic and manual designing. In most practical

1

cases, a large portion of the design time is spent on manual design, such as error checking and correction.

In recent years, highly interactive CAD systems have been developed to cope with this problem[1,2,3] and the design time has been reduced a great deal. However, its successful operation is fully dependent on the designer's ability. The designer carries out the design by employing his own specific knowledge of the layout. The expert designer must examine the wiring patterns carefully to modify or create wiring patterns for complete net connection. This is a time consuming and error prone procedure.

In the designing process, an essential difference between human beings and computer is an intuitive ability for reaching an appropriate goal. The ability is considered to be based on a mechanism of applying "rule of thumb" reasoning. Recently, several new CAD systems, based on artificial intelligence techniques have been reported[4,5]. However, it seems that there remain some difficulties in their use. Hajimu Mori and Keiko Mitsumoto realized an expert design system with PROLOG. The system applies the designer's specific knowledge to the designing process for residual path connections failed by preceding conventional wiring algorithms. Rules in PROLOG programs have a hierachical structure, and rules at the top level of the hierarchy can be considered as commands to the system. According to a specific situation, the designer inputs a rule name, and the interpreter interprets the program and produces a certain procedural sequence.

There are two major shortcomings in the system. Firstly, the designer's knowledge is not applied throughout the whole designing process. The system only applies rules in knowledge base to the remained unconnected nets. Secondly, users have to know the system's command functions. According to a specific situation, the designer inputs an appropriate rule name. So, the designer must have the knowledge of the command functions. The system proposed here is focused on the application of the designer's specific knowledge to the whole design process for practical routing design problem and relieves a designer from the burden of knowing the command functions. So, in the system we made changes both in knowledge representation and inference engine. The problem solving direction is similar to forward chaining except that the data or situation (in global database) evolves over time. In this case the next step is chosen either on the basis of new data or in response to a changed situation resulting from the last problem solving step taken. RES system has overcome the two major shortcomings mentioned above.

2. RES System

Until now, artificial intelligence techniques have been actively developed and CAD engineers hope to use them for their own purposes. In this routing system, the following key problems have to be clarified:

(1) Knowledge acquisition: Given a layout design situation, what kind of algorithms or operations will the designer perform to solve the problem?

(2) Knowledge representation: How should the designer's operation be represented in a knowledge-based form by a programming language?

(3) Problem solving strategy: How should the knowledge database be utilized or exploited to solve a specific problem?

A routing problem is to find a connecting path meeting all physical and electrical constrains for each given signal net. The connecting path is made by metal wires of different layers and via holes for interlayer connections. A signal net is a connection requirement to be electrically equivalent to a set of pins.

From the point of view of computational complexity, the routing problem is considered to be a hard combinatorial problem, in the sense that the computation time required to obtain the real optimum solution increases in exponential order as the problem size, i.e. number of signal nets, increases. Consequently, the routing algorithm is based on heuristic rationales. Although those heuristic algorithms have been improved year by year, they have not succeeded in producing a complete design in practical application. On the other hand, every algorithm has its restrictions. According to design circumstances algorithms should vary adaptively. For example, different structures or different size boards require different algorithms. In order to achieve 100% routing, the expert designer's "rule of thumb" should be used to calculate paths for residual connections failed by preceding routing algorithm.

We use micro-PROLOG as our implementing language, as it is a language suitable for knowledge representation and utilization. However, we made some changes to match our application. Mirco-PROLOG requires a huge amount of memory space, and mirco-PROLOG runs too slow on the conventional computer to be practically used. Therefore, we developed a predicate IRP which enables linkage of micro-PROLOG with PASCAL programs. Some problems remained to be solved. This additional function can compensate for the weak points of the conventional PROLOG and make it possible to take advantage of existing PASCAL programs.

Figure 1 shows a system architecture. The system includes three kinds of databases: knowledge base, global database, CAD database and procedure base. The global database stores a certain amount of design knowledge about specific situations. The CAD database contains layout design data. Knowledge base consists of design rules.

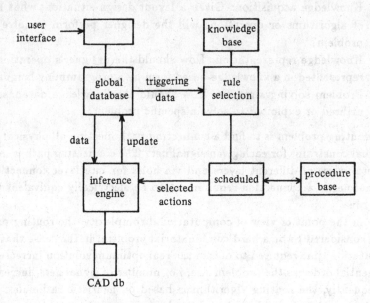

Fig. 1. RES system architecture

3. Knowledge Representation

RES provides a single global database which consists of a set of facts (goals). In micro-PROLOG a fact is represented in a list form: (p t1 t2 ... tn). P is a predicate, and ti is a term. The rules in RES are described as follows:

$$\langle rule \rangle ::= ((Rule \langle antecedent \rangle \langle consequent \rangle))$$

$$\langle antecedent \rangle ::= (\langle F \rangle)|(\langle F \rangle \langle antecedent \rangle)$$

$$\langle F \langle ::= (P \ t1 \ t2 \ ... tn)$$

$$\langle consequent \rangle ::= P$$

$$(P \ z) \rightarrow \langle action \rangle \langle action \rangle * \qquad \text{——— B}$$

$$\langle action \rangle ::= p$$

(Note: P is a predicate name, p is a procedure and "*" means this term may appear any number of times or not at all. In fact, line B is a rule in the PROLOG.)

4. Inference Engine

The RES interpreter executes a production system by performing the following operations:

(1) Determine which rules have satisfied antecedents.

   (This step is called match)

(2) Select one rule with a satisfied antecedent. If no rules satisfy antecedents, halt execution.

   (This step is called conflict resolution)

(3) Perform the actions of the selected rule.

   (This step is called act).

(4) Goto 1 (Go back to the first step).

This sequence of actions may be considered as the outline of a control structure that the user fills in as desired, for in RES the production system itself determines what control and problem-solving strategies will be used.

Control in a production system can be implemented using explicit goals, that is, elements in global database that designate desired states. Every rule's antecedent will be compared to match these explicit goals, and the first rule satisfied by these goals will be fired and executed.

In the following we will give the RES inference procedure implemented in micro-PROLOG:

```
((Routing1 z)
 (IF (search z2) ()
                ((PP Routing stops))))

((search 2)
 (Premise Rule Y)
 (unify Y)
 (findrule Rule Y X))

((Premise Rule Y)
 (Rule Y Z))

((unify ()))
((unify (X|Z))
       X
```

(unify Z))

((findrule Rule Y X)
(Rule Y X)
(X Z)
(search NEWGDB)).

5. Knowledge-Based Routing

As mentioned before, rules or design strategies can vary according to
different design circumstances. At present, we only deal with one kind of
PCB routing — all vias fixed.

The net connections are completed, pin-pair by pin-pair. The order
is very important because unconnected pin-pairs influence each other. To
determine which pin-pair should be tried first requires the know-how of
the designer. We want to connect the A's and B's with the only two vias
available being V1 and V2 (Fig. 2). Obviously the solution is to use V2 for
connecting the B's and V1 for connecting the A's, as shown in Fig. 3.

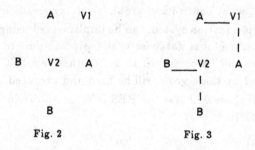

Fig. 2   Fig. 3

If the B's were attempted first, there would be no problem since it would
then find its only possible path, using V2 and A would have to use V1. It
is quite possible, however, that the A's would be attempted first.

If the A's are done first, then it depends on how the program logic is
set up in order to get the right solution. If it checks for the lower left via
first then it will find V2 and nothing will be left for the B's.

RES has the following knowledge database:

(1) Know what the different alternative paths for a pin pair are, i.e., if
we wish to decide which of the four possible paths a pin-pair should
take, obviously we must first know what these four possible paths
are.

```
((Rule (antecedent) AR2))
((AR2 Z)
    (initiative .)
    (inalset0   .)
    (inalset1   .)
    (inalset2   .)
    (changeGDB  .)
```

(Note: all rules presented in this paper are in simplified form. ChangeGDB stands for change global database).

Procedure initiative is used for initiative. Procedure inalset0 generates a pin-pair's all path occupying no vias, procedure inalset1 produces a pin-pair's all path occupying one via, and inalset2 with two vias.

(2) Be able to make valid judgements between alternative paths.

```
((Rule (antecedent) again))
((again Z))
    (select .)
    (CBA    .)
    (distribution .)
    (changeGDB .)).
```

Procedure select picks the connection yet to be routed with the smallest non-null alternative set. *IF* there is none, the process is complete. Procedure CBA evaluates the cost function on each member of the alternative set and picks the member with the minimum value. And procedure distribution confirms whether a selected path can be ultimately connected.

Due to increases in density, 100% completion rates are not easily obtained. Rip-up and reroute strategies can be applied to remove and reschedule wire segment that blocks a particular interconnection path (Fig. 4).

We may have the following operations to solve this problem.

step1. Find net B, which blocks the connection of net A.

step2. Delete the net B wires.

step3. Connect net A.

step4. Connect net B.

If step4 successes, the problem can be solved. But sometimes step4 may fail, due to net B has no other path to be found in current situation. In this case, we may solve the problem in the following steps (Fig. 5).

step1. Find out all the paths of net A, although some sources in the paths

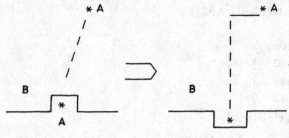

Fig. 4

have been occupied by other nets.

step2. Schedule all the paths of net A according to their occupied vias numbers and space needed.

step3. Select one path. If none left, halt execution.

step4. Get all the sources needed by the selected path, rip-up all the other connections that occupied some of these sources and reroute these connections including the selected path. If all the connections can be made, halt execution. If not, go to step3.

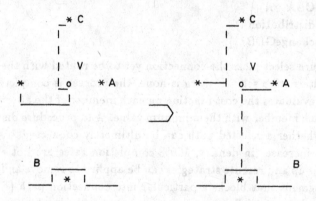

Fig. 5

There are also rules for pattern shape improvement. Wiring patterns are modified to have better shape by eliminating useless patterns like that shown in Fig. 6.

6. Conclusion

This paper presents a new routing system RES based on artificial intelligence techniques. We proposed, in a sense, a hybrid approach of combining the PROLOG and PASCAL languages. By doing so, we were able to con-

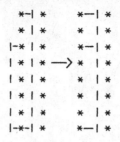

Fig. 6

struct a knowledge-based routing system which effectively takes advantage over an existing CAD system. The expert designer can store his own specific knowledge in the system and use it in the designing process.

In order to relieve the designer from the burden of having to know the usage of rules in knowledge base and to raise the degree of automatic designing process, we proposed a new inference mechanism instead of using PROLOG langauge's intrinsic inference mechanism. At the same time, we presents a knowledge representation method correspondingly.

References

1. F.D. Skinner, "Interative wiring system", *Proc. of 17th Design Automation Conference* (1980) 296-380.
2. H. Mori, T. Fujita, M. Annaka, S. Goto and T. Ohtsuki, "Advanced interactive layout design system for printed wiring boards", *Hardware and Software Concepts in VLSI*, ed. G. Rabbat, Van Nostran Reinhold, 1983.
3. S. Goto, T. Matsuda, K. Takamisawa, T. Fujita, H. Mizumura, H. Nakamura and K. Kitajima, "LAMBDA: An integrated master-slice LSI CAD system", *Integration* 1 (1983) 53-69.
4. L.I. Steinberg and T.M. Mitchell, "A knowledge based approach to VLSI CAD redesign system", *Proc. of 21th Design Automation Conference* (1984) 412-418.
5. H. Mori, K. Mitsumoto, T. Fujita, S. Goto and H. Wakata, *WIREX: VLSI Wiring Design Expert System Technical Memorandum*, ICOT Research Center, 1985.

FORMALIZING AND AUTOMATING THE SOFTWARE PROCESS THROUGH SUCCESSIVE REFINEMENT

Dai Min & Xu Jiafu
Institute of Computer Software
Nanjing University

Abstract

FASP (Formalization and Automation of the Software Process) methodology is proposed in this paper. It is based on the stepwise principle and adopts the FASP tree structure for the formal description of the whole software development process, from requirement analysis, functional specification, global design to detailed algorithm and data structure design. The upper levels of a FASP tree can be understood by non DP professionals while the lower levels can automatically be transformed to executable codes. Automatic detection of interface errors can also be supported with FASP.

1. Introduction

It has been almost 20 years since the word "software engineering appeared. But the crisis still exists[1]. The long development life cycle, unsatisfying product quality and difficulties in understanding and maintaining the resulting software, etc. are serious problems in the present situation. Many new and original methods and techniques have been proposed in recent software engineering practice, but they are not so popular as we expect. One of the reasons is the complex theoretical basis underlying these methods and techniques and the difficulties encountered in management by programmers when practising them. Perhaps, what we need is some conceptually simple and flexible methods and techniques which can help programmers to avoid errors, omissions and inconsistencies as fully as possible and provide a way to understand the resulting implemented systems. This motivates the research of FASP methodology.

In this paper, we will introduce the main ideas and description method of FASP methodology, its support for the whole development process and automation of part of the process. Although the examples illustrated are based on PASCAL, in fact, FASP methodology can be used in any software development process in which any programming language or computable specification language is used.

2. FASP Ideas and Description Method

FASP is a formal software methodology for software development process. It adopts the familiar and well-understood tree structure, called FASP tree, as a formal description form, in which nodes may have any definite number of branches. Initially, the root records the broadest functional specification. It is refined every time when the tree is extended to comprise a new level, such a stepwise development process continues until all the leaf nodes are executable statements or necessary data declarations. Nodes which have the same direct ancestor imply an execution sequence from the left to the right. In order to record the software process the following notations are used in FASP trees.

○ :an ordinary node which may record specifications and data declarations of various degrees of details and all the executable statements;

○ :a loop node, in which loop conditions are described;

╱ :an undirected edge which indicates that the operations in the subnode which it connects will unconditionally be performed;

╱ :a directed edge with a downward arrow, representing the conditions to perform node operations;

╱ :a directed edge with an upward arrow, indicating data visibility (see below).

For example, the FASP tree in Fig. 1(a) means that the functions of node *A* can be illustrated in two statements; *B*; if P then *C* else *D*; while the FASP tree of Fig.1(b) is equal to the loop program segment:

```
while p do
begin
    A;
    B;
    if p1 then C
```

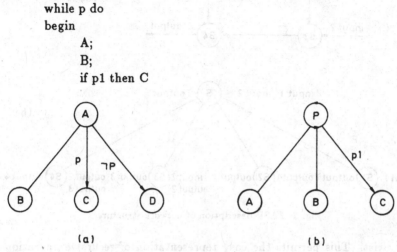

(a)   (b)

Fig. 1. Two simple FASP trees

The execution sequence in a FASP tree implies that nodes on the left can produce data for those on the right in the same level, but this is not compulsory. If there is no such a data dependency, parallel execution will be possible. Thus, FASP trees can be flexibly used to describe both sequential and parallel computations. In general, any relationship among function modules described using network structure[2] can also be described using FASP tree structure. Fig. 2 gives an example where (b) is a FASP equivalent representation of (a) and nodes *S*2 and *S*3 in (a) can be executed in parallel because there is no data dependency.

In the completed FASP tree of a particular software, leaf nodes can only include primitive operations and data declarations which need no further refinement (such as assignment statements, skip and variable declarations, etc. in traditional programming languages), an existing FASP structure name (it may be part of the current design) and some standard external programs which are not developed with FASP methodology. To determine whether a node needs further refinement, it depends on the syntax of formal inputs received by the code generator used (see section 4). When the name of an existing FASP tree is used elsewhere, the inputs and outputs of it must be explicitly declared on the left and right of its root respectively, if

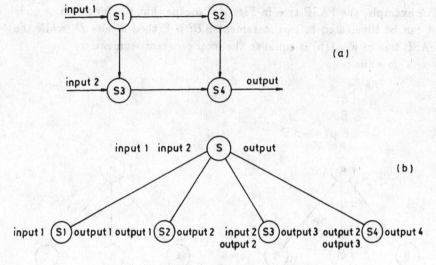

Fig. 2. FASP description of network structure.

they exist. This permits the easy representation of recursive operations. For instance, factorial function can be recursively defined by a FASP tree (see Fig. 3).

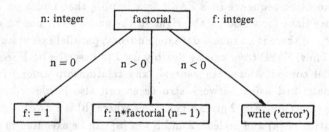

Fig. 3. The FASP tree of factorial function.

FASP methodoloy can also support the stepwise refinement design of data structures in the same way as they are used in the development of system functions (see the knight's tour example in the next section). Data visibility is determined by the position where data declarations appear. A data declaration is in the unit of a tree (or subtree) and it must appear in the left most branch (subtree) of its scope tree (or subtree). Such a scope is denoted by a directed edge with an upward arrow between the root of the scope tree and its left most subtree. Fig. 4 is an example illustrating data visibility, where the scope of variable a is the tree rooted A while that

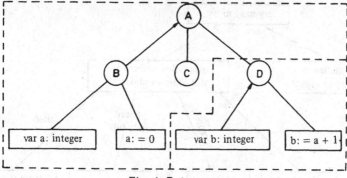

Fig. 4. Data scope

of *b* is the subtree rooted *D*.

One of the obvious advantages of FASP methodology is the use of a unique FASP tree structure for the description of the whole software process instead of various specification languages for different phases adopted in traditional software life cycle. This avoids the burden of understanding and transforming between different languages. Thus the software developed are more easy to understand and maintain.

3. Support for the Whole Development Process

In this section we take the well-known knight's tour problem for example to illustrate how the whole development process can be recorded with FASP methodology.

The problem can be described as follows:

Given a $n*n$ board with $n*n$ fields. A knight — being allowed to move according to the rules of chess — is placed on an initial field. The problem is to find a covering of the entire board, if there exists one, i.e., to compute a tour of $n*n-1$ moves such that every field of the board is visited exactly once.

The obvious way to solve the problem of covering $n*n$ fields is to consider the problem of either performing a next move or finding out that none is possible. Let us therefore define a backtracking algorithm trying to perform a next move. A first broadest FASP tree description is shown in Fig. 5.

If we wish to be more precise in describing this algorithm we must make some decisions on data representations. An obvious step is to represent the board by a matrix, say *h*, and the occupation of field by an integer to keep track of the history of successive board occupations. Their PASCAL

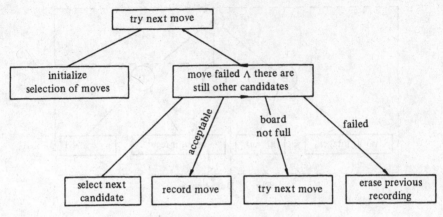

Fig. 5. The broadest FASP tree of the algorithm.

declarations are

$$\text{type} \qquad \text{index} = 1..n;$$
$$\text{var} \qquad h: \text{array [index, index] of integer};$$

where

$$h[x,y] = 0: \quad \text{field } \langle x,y \rangle \text{ has not been visited};$$
$$h[x,y] = i: \quad \text{field } \langle x,y \rangle \text{ has been visited in the } i\text{th move}$$
$$(1 \leq i \leq n * n).$$

The next decision concerns the choice of appropriate parameters to determine the starting conditions for the next move and also to report on its success. The former task is solved by specifying the coordinates x, y from which the move is to be made and by specifying the number i of the move (for recording purpose). The latter task requires a boolean result parameter; q=true denotes success; q=false failure. Moreover, we introduce two local variables u and v to stand for the coordinates of possible destinations determined according to the jump pattern of knights and another $q1$ as the result parameter in the recursive call of this algorithm. Then Fig. 5 is made more detailed in Fig. 6, in which control conditions must exhaust the possibilities. For example, the predicate "acceptable" can be expressed as the logical combination of the conditions that the new field lies on the board, i.e., $1 \leq u \leq n$ and $1 \leq v \leq n$, and that it has not been visited previously, i.e., $h[u,v] = 0$. The operation of recording the possible move is expressed by the assignment $h[u,v] := i$. At the same time, the primitive operation "back" to perform when "not acceptable" should be attached to the FASP tree, denoting a stop to the current loop body and return back to discriminate loop conditions.

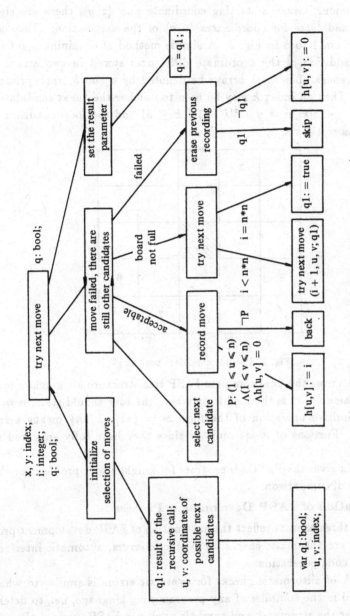

Fig. 6. The detailed FASP tree

Just one more refinement step to determine u and v will lead us to final expression. Given a starting coordinate pair $\langle x, y \rangle$, there are eight potential candidates for coordinates $\langle u, v \rangle$ of the destination. They are numbered from 1 to 8 in Fig. 7. A simple method of obtaining u, v from x, y is by addition of the coordinate differences stored in two arrays of single differences. Let these arrays be denoted by a and b, appropriately initialized. Then an index k may be used to number the "next candidate". Thus, $u = x + a[k], v = y + b[k]$, $(1 \leq k \leq 8)$ and the loop condition is expressed as $\neg q1 \wedge k < 8$.

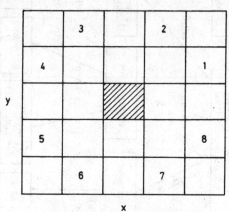

Fig. 7. Possible candidate positions

Figure 8 shows the final complete FASP tree structure for knight's tour problem, where $\langle 1, 1 \rangle$ is the field from where the tour should start, $n = 5$, and the primitive operation of the form $z := \{s1, \ldots, sn\}$ means array assignment. Portions of it are omitted since they have fully appeared in Fig. 6.

Appendix gives the PASCAL program for knight's tour problem for the convenience of comparison.

4. Automation of FASP Development Process

At least three aspects reflect the automation of FASP development process. There are automatic checks for syntactic errors, automatic interface control and code generation.

The work of aurormatic checks for syntactic errors is similar to what accomplished in the compiler of any programming language, i.e., to determine whether the structures and symbols used in a FASP tree are allowed by FASP methodology and all the identifiers are appropriately declared before use, etc.

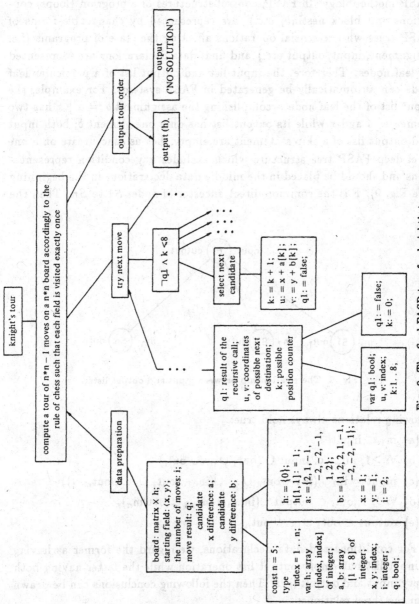

Fig. 8. The final FASP tree for knight's tour.

Automatic interface control is one of the important characterisics of FASP methodology. In FASP, control structures of a program (loops, conditions and block nesting, etc.) are represented by changeable forms of FASP trees while essential operations affecting the state of programs (i.e. assignment, input/output etc.) and final data declarations are represented by leaf nodes. Therefore, the input list and output list of a particular leaf node can automatically be generated in FASP systems. For example, the input list of the leaf node accomplishing the assignment $b := a + x$ has two elements: a and x while its output list has only one element b; both input and output list of a skip statement are empty. Let us concentrate on a one level deep FASP tree structure which excludes any condition representations and should be placed in the middle data declarations in the beginning (see Fig. 9). F is the common direct ancestor of nodes $S1$ to Sn. Then the

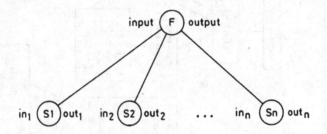

Fig. 9. The relationship between input and output lists

following relations always hold true:

(a) $in_1 \subset$ input

(b) $\forall i \geq 1$, $in_{i+1} \subset$ input $\cup$ (out$_1$ $\cup \ldots \cup$ out$_i$)

(c) input $= in_1 \cup (in_2 -$ out$_1$ $\cup \ldots \cup (in_n - (out_1$ $\cup \ldots \cup$out$_{n-1}))$

(d) $\forall i \geq 1$, out$_i \subset$ output $\cup (in_{i+1} \cup in_{i+2} \cup \ldots \cup in_n)$,

(e) output $\subset$ out$_1$ $\cup \ldots \cup$ out$_n$

For conditions and data declarations, we regard the former as having an input list but empty output list operation while the latter having both empty input and output lists. Then the following conclusions can be drawn from the three relations:

(a) Each element in the input list of any leaf node in a final FASP tree is either a constant or produced by at least one leaf node on its left which has no exclusive condition with it in execution.

(b) Each element in the output list of any leaf node either appears in one or more input lists of leaf nodes and final conditions on its right or contributes to the output result of the system;

(c) Each element in the final conditions is either a constant or produced by some leaf nodes on its left.

Once these relations are not satisfied in a final FASP tree, interface errors appear. FASP systems will automaticity complete the interface error detection and report the possible error positions to users. Such a way of error detection is also helpful for the discovery of inconsistencies and omissions in the previous specifications, which ease the work of maintenance.

Code generation can be accomplished in various ways. A simple way is to travel a FASP tree in some order and generate the corresponding codes at the same time. For example, Fig. 10 gives a FASP tree produced by a preorder traversal, i.e., visit root first and then the subtrees from the left to the right. In a particular FASP system, there may be several code generators, each accepting a different style description language as its formal input and generating codes for a lot of machines. This makes FASP methodology more elegant and flexible to use.

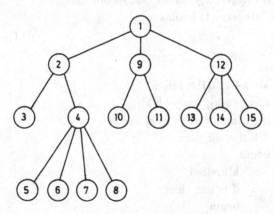

Fig. 10. FASP tree traversal

5. Conclusions

The research of FASP methodology will continue further in Nanjing University. Our experience indicates that graphical structures like FASP trees are preferable to other specification languages for the description of software development process. A FASP tree has a simple structure, flexible form and it is easy to use. It is a common language between programmers and non DP professionals. Its ability to record not only programs but also the development process provides a way to understand the implemented systems. We believe that FASP methodology will contribute to the effort of avoiding some of the unnecessary problems in software engineering[1].

Appendix. PASCAL program for the knight's tour problem[3]

```
program knightstour (output);
const
      n=5;   nsq=25;
type
      index = 1..n;
var
      i, j: index;
      q: boolean;
      s: set of index;
      a,b: array [1..8] of integer;
      h: array[index, index] of integer;
procedure try(i: integer; x,y: index; var q: boolean);
      var k,u,v: integer; q1: boolean;
      begin
            k:=0;
            repeat
                k:=k+1; q1:= false;
                u:=x+a[k]; v:=y+b[k];
                if (u in s) and (v in s) then
                if h[u,v]=0 then
                begin
                      h[u,v]:=i;
                      if i<nsq then
                      begin
                            ry (i+1, u, v, q1);
                            if not q1 then h[u,v]:=0
                      end
                      else q1:=true
                end
            until q1 or (k=8);
            q:=q1
```

```
        end (try);
begin
        s:=[1,2,3,4,5,];
        a[1]:=2; b[1]:=1;
        a[2]:=1; b[2]:=2;
        a[3]:=-1; b[3]:=2;
        a[4]:=-2; b[4]:= 1;
        a[5]:=-2; b[5]:=1;
        a[6]:=-1; b[6]:= -2;
        a[7]:=1; b[7]:= -2;
        a[8]:=2; b[8]:=-1;
        for i:= 1 to n do
            for j:=1 to n do
                h[i, j]:= 0;
        h[1, i]:=1; try(2,1,1,q);
        if q then
            for i:=1 to n do
            begin
                for j:=1 to n do write(h[i, j]:5);
                writeln
            end
        else writeln('NO SOLUTION')
end.
```

References

1. J. Martin, *An Information Systems Manifesto*, Prentice-Hall, 1984.
2. *Proceedings of the 8th International Conference on Software Engineering*, London, UK, (August 28-30 1985) 68-74.
3. Niklaus Wirth, *Algorithm + Data Structure = Programs*, Prentice-Hall, 1976.

A NEW ATTRIBUTE GRAMMAR CLASS
— DEPENDENT ATTRIBUTE GRAMMAR

Tang Changqing

Institute of Software Technology, Academia Sinica

Abstract

This paper puts forward a new attribute grammar class — dependent attribute grammar (DAG). The checking algorithm for this class depends polynomially in time on the size of input AGs. The class of DAG contains the class of OAG. A semantic analyzer generator based on DAG has been built.

1. Introduction

For the past decade, many developments of AGs had been made, and various classes of AGs had been raised[1,2,4,5]. At the same time, some compiler generators based on the classes of AGs had been constructed[3,6].

One of the problem of AGs is to find some practical algorithms to study greater classes of AGs. Although a lot of effort has been made to obtain such algorithms, some of them restrict the classes of acceptable AGs severely such as L-AG and others are very complex in time such as ANCAG. The algorithm for OAG[2] is simple, but the algorithm for checking circles and the algorithm for computing visit-sequences are mixed together. Therefore, the class of OAG is smaller. This paper puts forward a new attribute grammar class — dependent attribute grammar (DAG). The checking algorithm for its class depends polynomially in time on the size of input AGs and the class of DAG contains the class of OAG.

2. The Definition of AGs
Definition 2.1.

The model G can be called attribute grammar (AG) if and only if G has the following five properties:

(1) G has a semantic domain D,

$$D = (\Omega_D, \emptyset_D)$$

where $\Omega_D = \{v | v \text{ is a value domain}\}$,

$$\emptyset_D = \{F | F : v_{k+1} \times \ldots \times v_m \to v_0 \times \ldots \times v_k$$
$$\text{where } v_i \in \Omega_D, \text{ for } i \in [0..m]\}.$$

(2) G has a context-free grammar G_0,

$$G_0 = (V_t, V_n, P, Z)$$

where V_t is the set of terminal nodes, V_n is the set of non-terminal nodes, Z is the beginning node. The node set is $V, V = V_t \cup V_n$. The capital letters are used to represent non-terminal nodes, small letters to represent terminal nodes, and letter N indicates a general reference to nodes. P is the set of productions. A production $p, p \in P$, can be indicated as,

$$p : N_0 ::= N_1 \ldots N_{n_p}$$

where $n_p \geq 0, N_i \in V$, for all $i \in [0..n_p]$.

(3) Each node $N, N \in V$, has attributes, and they are denoted by $A(N)$. These attributes $A(N)$ can be divided into two parts: synthesized attributes $S(N)$ and inherited attributes $I(N)$, such that $A(N) = S(N) \cup I(N)$ and $S(N) \cap I(N) = \emptyset$.

Small letters with a bar above them are used to represent attributes and dot to link the attribute with the node it belongs to. For example, $N.\bar{a}$ represents that node N has as attribute $\bar{a}$.

(4) For each attribute $\bar{a}$, the set of the possible values of $\bar{a}$ is denoted by $v(\bar{a})$. Ω_D contains value domain v such that $v = v(\bar{a})$.

(5) With each production $p, p \in P$,

$$p : N_0 ::= N_1 \ldots N_{n_p}, n_p \geq 0$$

is associated to a finite set r_p of semantic rules which have the following form:

$$(N_{i_0}.\bar{a}_0, \ldots, N_{i_k}.\bar{a}_k) = F(N_{i_{k+1}}.\bar{a}_{k+1}, \ldots, N_{i_m}.\bar{a}_m)$$

where for $j \in [0..m], i_j \in [0..n_p]$, and $F \in \emptyset_D$,

$$F : v_{k+1} \times \ldots \times v_m \rightarrow v_0 \times \ldots v_k,$$

such that $v_j = v(N_{i_j}.\bar{a}_j)$ for all $j \in [0..m]$.

When the identifier of the node is not important, the semantic rule is simply denoted by

$$(\bar{a}_0, \ldots, \bar{a}_k) = F(\bar{a}_{k+1}, \ldots, \bar{a}_m).$$

Definition 2.2.

G is an AG. p is a production, $p \in P$,

$$p : N_0 ::= N_1 \ldots N_{n_p}, n_p \geq 0,$$

then its attribute occurence set $A(p)$ can be defined as,

$$A(p) = \{\bar{a} | \bar{a} \in a(N_i), \quad 0 \leq i \leq n_p\},$$

and its inherited attribute occurence set $I(p)$ and its synthesized attribute occurence set $S(p)$ can be defined respectively as follows:

$$I(p) = \{\bar{a} | \bar{a} \in I(N_i), \quad 0 \leq i \leq n_p\},$$
$$S(p) = \{\bar{a} | \bar{a} \in S(N_i), \quad 0 \leq i \leq n_p\}.$$

Definition 2.3.

G is an AG. F is a semantic rule with the following form,

$$(\bar{a}_0, \ldots, \bar{a}_k) = F(\bar{a}_{k+1} \ldots, \bar{a}_m),$$

then its defining attribute occurrence set $DS(F)$ and applied attribute occurrence set $US(F)$ can be defined respectively as,

$$DS(F) = \{\bar{a}_i | 0 \leq i \leq k\},$$
$$US(F) = \{\bar{a}_i | k+1 \leq i \leq m\}.$$

Definition 2.4.

G is an AG. F is a semantic rule, $F \in \Omega_D$, with the following form,

$$(\bar{a}_0, \ldots, \bar{a}_k) = F(\bar{a}_{k+1}, \ldots, \bar{a}_m).$$

If for each attribute $\bar{a}, \bar{a} \in US(F)$, there exists a value $a', a' \in v(\bar{a})$, where a' is assigned to attribute a, then semantic rule F is said to be determined and has a value F_{val} as follows:

$$F_{val} = (a_0', \ldots, a_k') = F(a_{k+1}', \ldots, a_m'),$$

where $a_i' \in v(\bar{a})$, for $i \in [0..m]$. Each component of F_{val} can be denoted by $F_{\bar{a}}, \bar{a} \in DS(F)$. That is,

$$F_{val} = (F_{\bar{a}_0}, \ldots, F_{\bar{a}_k}) = F(a_{k+1}', \ldots, a_m').$$

If $DS(F) = \{\bar{a}\}$, then F_{val} can be simply denoted by $F_{\bar{a}}$.

In order to describe the properties of AGs and the algorithms related to AGs conveniently, we will introduce a new kind of graph — attribute graph.

Definition 2.5.

The attribute graph GR is a four-tuple,

$$GR = (ND, SL, AL, RT)$$

where ND is the node set of GR, SL is the structure relation set of GR, AL is the attribute relation set of GR, and RT is the root of GR. They are defined respectively as follows:

$ND = \{N|N$ is called node of GR, it is denoted by a rectangular box in which there are some characters called attribute of node $N.\}$;

$SL = \{\langle N_1, N_2 \rangle | N_1, N_2 \in ND$, and in GR, N_1 is above N_2 and there is a dashline between N_1 and $N_2.\}$;

$AL = \{(\bar{a}, \bar{b}) | \bar{a}, \bar{b}$ are respectively the attribute of N_1 and the attribute of $N_2, N_1, N_2 \in ND$ and there is a directed arc from $\bar{a}$ to $\bar{b}.\}$;

$RT = N$ where $N \in ND$ and there is no N' such that $N' \in ND$ and $\langle N', N \rangle \in SL$.

There is no isolated node in the attribute graph GR, that is, in GR,
(a) $ND = \{N\}$, or
(b) for all $N, N \in ND$, there exists $N', N' \in ND$, such that $\langle N, N' \rangle \in SL$ or $\langle N', N \rangle \in SL$.

The components of GR can be respectively denoted by $ND(GR), SL(GR), AL(GR)$ and $RT(GR)$.

Definition 2.6.

GR is an attribute graph. Its closure GR^+ is also an attribute graph and can be defined as,

$$GR^+ = (ND, SL, AL, RT)$$

where $ND = ND(GR)$;
   $SL = SL(GR)$;
   $AL = AL(GR) \cup \{(\bar{a}, \bar{b})|$ there is a route from $\bar{a}$ to $\bar{b}$ in $GR\}$;
   $RT = RT(GR)$.

Definition 2.7.

GR is an attribute graph. If, in GR, there is a route from attribute $\bar{a}$ to itself, there is a circle in GR.

3. The Dependent Attribute Grammar
Definition 3.1.

G is an AG. Its dependent graph set $DG(G)$ can be defined as follows:

$$DG(G) = \{D(p)|p \in P\}$$

where $D(p)$ is the dependent graph of a production p,

$$p : N_0 ::= N_1 \ldots N_{n_p}, \quad n_p \geq 0,$$

and can be defined as

$$D(p) = (ND, SL, AL, RT),$$

where $ND = \{N_i|0 \leq i \leq n_p\}$;
   $SL = \{\langle N_0, N_i \rangle| \quad 1 \leq i \leq n_p\}$;
   $AL = \{(\bar{a}, \bar{b})|\exists F \in r_p, \bar{a} \in US(F), \bar{b} \in DS(F)\}$;
   $RT = N_0$.

Definition 3.2.

G is an AG. Its production dependent graph set $PDS(G)$ can be defined as

$$PDS(G) = \{PD(p)|p \in P\}$$

where $PD(p)$ is the production dependent graph of production p,

$$p : N_0 ::= N_1 \ldots N_{n_p}, \quad n_p \geq 0,$$

and can be defined as follows:

$$PD(p) = (ND, SL, AL, RT)^+,$$

where $ND = ND(D(p))$;

$SL = SL(D(p))$;

$AL = AL(D(p)) \cup \{(N_i.\bar{a}, N_i.\bar{b})|$ for all $i, i \in [0..n_p]$,

$\exists p' \in P, p' : N_0' ::= N_1' \ldots N_{n_{p'}}'$

$n_{p'} \geq 0$, such that $\exists j \in [0..n_{p'}]$,

$N_j' = N_i$ and

$(N_j'.\bar{a}, N_j'.\bar{b}) \in AL(PD(p'))\}$;

$RT = RT(D(p))$.

Definition 3.3.

G is an AG. G is called dependent attribute grammar (DAG) if and only if for all production $p, p \in P$, there is no circle in the production dependent graph $PD(p)$.

Example 3.1.

G is an AG. G is composed of

$V_n = \{W, X, Y\}$;

$V_t = \{t, s\}$;

$Z = W$;

$W : \bar{a}(S); \quad X : \bar{a}(I), \quad \bar{b}(S), \quad \bar{c}(I), \quad \bar{d}(S)$;

$Y : \bar{e}(I), \quad \bar{f}(S), \quad \bar{g}(I), \quad \bar{h}(S); \quad t : \bar{n}(I); \quad s : \bar{m}(I)$;

$p_1 : W ::= XY$;

$r_{p_1} : W.\bar{a} = F_1(X.\bar{b}, Y.\bar{f}); \quad X.\bar{a} = F_2(Y.\bar{h}); \quad X.\bar{c} = F_3(\ )$;

$\quad\quad Y.\bar{e} = F_4(X.\bar{d}); \quad Y.\bar{g} = F_5(\ )$;

$p_2 : X ::= t$;

$r_{p_2} : X.\bar{b} = F_6(t.\bar{n}); \quad X.\bar{d} = F_7(X.\bar{c}, t.\bar{n})$;

$p_3 : Y ::= s$;

$r_{p_3} : Y.\bar{f} = F_8(s.\bar{m}); \quad Y.\bar{h} = F_9(Y.\bar{g}, s.\bar{m})$.

The dependent graph set $DG(G)$, and the production dependent graph set $PDS(G)$ are shown in Fig. 3.1. From the figure, we know that G belongs to DAG. However, G does not belong to OAG^2.

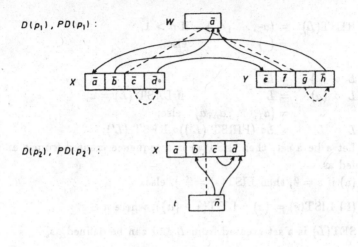

$D(p_1), PD(p_1)$:

$D(p_2), PD(p_2)$:

$D(p_3), PD(p_3)$:

Fig. 3.1. $DG(G)$ is denoted by real directed arcs and $PDS(G)$ by real and dash directed arcs.

4. The Operation Sequence

As the definition given above of the production dependent graph $PD(p)$ of a production p, $PD(p)$ completely reflects all direct and indirect dependent relations among attributes associated with the nodes in the production p. Therefore, we can compute the operation sequences from these dependent relations. For the convenience of describing, we introduce some operators in sequence.

Definition 4.1.

Let L be a sequence, $L = (a_1, a_2, \ldots, a_n), n \geq 0$. Some operators on L can be defined as follows.

(1) FIRST(L) $= a_1$ if $n > 0$,
               $= \wedge$ else;

(2) LAST(L) $= a_n$ if $n > 0$,
               $= \wedge$ else;

(3) $\text{REST}(L)$ $= (a_2, \ldots, a_n)$ if $n > 1$,

$= (\ )$ else;

(4) $L \circ (\ )$ $= L$,

$L \circ (a)$ $= L$ if $\text{LAST}\ (L) = a$,

$= (a_1, \ldots, a_n, a)$ else;

$L \circ L'$ $= L\circ (\text{FIRST}\ (L'))\circ \text{REST}\ (L')$;

(5) Let s be a set, then $\text{LIST}(s)$ is a sequence created from s and can be defined as,

(a) if $s = \emptyset$, then $\text{LIST}(s) = (\ )$, else

(b) $\text{LIST}(s) = (a) \circ \text{LIST}(s - \{a\})$, where $a \in s$.

(6) $\text{SET}(L)$ is a set created from L and can be defined as,

(a) if $L = (\ )$, then
$\text{SET}\ (L) = \emptyset$, else

(b) $\text{SET}\ (L) = \text{FIRST}(L) \cup \text{SET}(\text{REST}(L))$.

Definition 4.2.

G is an AG. Let p be a production, $p \in P$. If there is no circle in the production dependent graph $PD(p)$, then attribute sequence $AS(p)$ of production p can be defined as

$$AS(p) = \text{LIST}(APS_{p,i}) \circ \ldots \circ \text{LIST}(APS_{p,m})$$

where $APS_{p,i}$ is the attribute partition subset and can be defined as follows:

$$APS_{p,2n+1} = \{\bar{a}|\bar{a} \in I(p), \bar{a} \notin \bigcup_{i=1}^{2n} APS_{p,i},$$

and there is no $\bar{b}, \bar{b} \in A(p)$,

such that $(\bar{b}, \bar{a}) \in AL(PD(p))$

and $\bar{b} \notin \bigcup_{i=1}^{2n} APS_{p,i}\}$;

$$APS_{p,2n+2} = \{\bar{a}|\bar{a} \in S(p), \bar{a} \notin \bigcup_{i=1}^{2n+1} APS_{p,i},$$

and there is no $\bar{b}, \bar{b} \in A(p)$,

such that $(\bar{b}, \bar{a}) \in AL(PD(p))$

and $\bar{b} \notin \bigcup_{i=1}^{2n+1} APS_{p,i}\}$;

where $n \geq 0$, and

(a) $A(p) = \bigcup\limits_{i=1}^{m} APS_{p,i}, \ m \geq 1,$

(b) if $j \neq k, \ j, k \in [1..m]$, then $APS_{p,j} \cap APS_{p,k} = \emptyset$.

Definition 4.3.

G is an AG. If G belongs to DAG, then its attribute sequence table $AST(G)$ can be defined as,

$$AST(G) = \{(p, AS(p) | p \in P\}.$$

Definition 4.4.

G is an AG. If its attribute sequence table $AST(G)$ exists, then its instruction sequence table $IST(G)$ can be defined as

$$IST(G) = \{(p, IS(p) | p \in P\}$$

where $IS(p)$ is the instruction sequence of production p,

$$p : N_0 ::= N_1 \ldots N_{n_p}, \quad n_p \geq 0,$$

and can be defined as follows:

$$IS(p) = ACI(AS(p)),$$

where $ACI(L)$ is a transfering function which transfers attribute sequence L to the corresponding instruction sequence and can be defined as follows:

(1) if $L = (\ )$ then $ACI(L) = (\uparrow)$, else

(2) $ACI(L) = DO((\text{FIRST}(L)) \circ ACI(\text{REST}(L))$,

    where $DO(\bar{a})$ is a transfering function which transfer attribute $\bar{a}$ to the corresponding instruction and can be defined as follows:

    (a) if $\bar{a} \in S(N_0), \exists F \in r_p, \bar{a} \in DS(F)$, then
        $DO(\bar{a}) = (F_{\text{val}})$;

    (b) if $\bar{a} \in I(N_0)$, then
        $DO(\bar{a}) = (\uparrow) \ \exists \bar{b} \in A(p), (\bar{b}, \bar{a}) \in AL(PD(p))$,
        $= (\ )$ other cases;

    (c) if $\bar{a} \in A(N_i), N_i \in V_t$, where $i \in [1..n_p]$, then
        $DO(\bar{a}) = (\ )$;

    (d) if $\bar{a} \in I(N_i), N_i \in V_n$, where $i \in [1..n'_p]$, and $\exists F \in r_p, \bar{a} \in DS(F)$,
        $DO(\bar{a}) = (F_{\text{val}})$;

(e) if $\bar{a} \in S(N_i)$, $N_i \in V_n$, where $i \in [1..n_p]$, then
$$DO(\bar{a}) = (\downarrow_{N_i});$$

(f) Other case,
$$DO(\bar{a}) = (\ ).$$

In the above, '$\uparrow$', '$\downarrow_{N_i}$' respectively specify returning to the father node and visiting son node N_i.

Definition 4.5.

G is an AG. If its instruction sequence table $IST(G)$ exists, then its driving sequence table $DST(G)$ can be defined as

$$DST(G) = \{(p, DV(p)) | p \in P\}$$

where $DV(p)$ is the driving sequence of production p, and can be defined as follows:

$$DV(p) = (S_{p,1}) \circ ICD(IS(p), S_{p,1})$$

where $S_{p,i}$ is the state identifier and $ICD(L, S_{p,i})$ is a transfering function which transfers instruction sequence L to the corresponding driving sequence. It can be defined as,

(1) if $L = (\ )$, then
$$ICD(L, S_{p,i}) = (;\ );$$

(2) if $L \neq (\ )$, then
  (a) if FIRST$(L) \neq$ '$\uparrow$', '$\downarrow_N$', then
  $$ICD(L, S_{p,i}) = (\text{FIRST}(L)) \circ ICD\ (\text{REST}(L), S_{p,i});$$
  (b) if FIRST$(L) =$ '$\uparrow$' or '$\downarrow_N$', then
  $$ICD(L, S_{p,i}) = (\text{FIRST}(L), ;, S_{p,i+1}) \circ ICD(\text{REST}(L), S_{p,i+1}).$$

Now we may build a semantic analyzer for an attribute grammar G by using the driving sequence table mentioned above. This semantic analyzer has the table-driving structure. That is, it looks over the driving sequence table according to a given state and executes the driving sequence corresponding to that state.

Example 4.1.

The attribute sequence table $AST(G)$ and the driving sequence table $DST(G)$ of G in Example 3.1 are respectively shown in Fig. 4.1 and Fig. 4.2.

$$p_1 \quad (X.\bar{c}, \; Y.\bar{g}, \; X.\bar{b}, \; X.\bar{d}, \; Y.\bar{f}, \; Y.\bar{h}, \; X.\bar{a}, \; Y.\bar{e}, \; W.\bar{a})$$
$$p_2 \quad (X.\bar{a}, \; X.\bar{c}, \; X.\bar{b}, \; X.\bar{d})$$
$$p_3 \quad (Y.\bar{e}, \; Y.\bar{g}, \; Y.\bar{f}, \; Y.\bar{h})$$

Fig. 4.1. The attribute sequence table $AST(G)$ of G in Example 3.1.

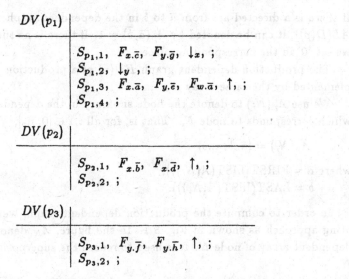

$$DV(p_1)$$

$$S_{p_1,1}, \quad F_{x.\bar{c}}, \quad F_{y.\bar{g}}, \quad \downarrow_x, \; ;$$
$$S_{p_1,2}, \quad \downarrow_y, \; ;$$
$$S_{p_1,3}, \quad F_{x.\bar{a}}, \quad F_{y.\bar{e}}, \quad F_{w.\bar{a}}, \quad \uparrow, \; ;$$
$$S_{p_1,4}, \; ;$$

$$DV(p_2)$$

$$S_{p_2,1}, \quad F_{x.\bar{b}}, \quad F_{x.\bar{d}}, \quad \uparrow, \; ;$$
$$S_{p_2,2}, \; ;$$

$$DV(p_3)$$

$$S_{p_3,1}, \quad F_{y.\bar{f}}, \quad F_{y.\bar{h}}, \quad \uparrow, \; ;$$
$$S_{p_3,2}, \; ;$$

Fig. 4.2. The driving sequence table $DST(G)$ of G in Example 3.1.

5. Its Algorithm and Complexity

In this section, we give an algorithm which checks whether a given AG belongs to DAG and computes the operation sequences. The algorithm depends polynomially in time on the size of the input AG. The parameters used are:

$|P|$— the number of productions;
$|R|$— the maximum number of nodes in a single production;
$|X|$— the maximum number of attributes associated with a single node;
$|V|$— the number of nodes;
$|G| = |P||R|$— the length of AG;
$|D| = |P||X|$— the maximum number of attributes in a dependent graph of a production.

The dependent graph mentioned above are implemented by an array —

dependent array in practice. For a production $p, p \in P$,

$$p : N_0 ::= N_i \ldots N_{n_p}, \quad n_p \geq 0,$$

then its dependent array A_p can be defined as,

$$AO = \text{LIST}(A(N_0)) \circ \text{LIST}(A(N_i)) \circ \ldots \circ \text{LIST}(A(N_n)),$$
$$A_p = (AO, AO).$$

If there is a directed arc from $\overline{a}$ to $\overline{b}$ in the dependent graph $D(p)$, $(\overline{a}, \overline{b}) \in AL(D(p))$, it can be denoted by $A_p(\overline{a}, \overline{b}) = 1$. If there is no such direct arc, we set '0' in the corresponding place.

The production dependent graph $PD(p)$ of a production p can be implemented by the same array A_p.

We use $A_p(N_i)$ to denote the node subarray in the dependent array A_p, which corresponds to node N_i. That is, for all $i, i \in [0..n_p]$,

$$A_p(N_i) = (\overline{a}..\overline{b}, \overline{a}..\overline{b})$$

where $\overline{a} = \text{FIRST}(\text{LIST}(A(N_i)))$,
   $\overline{b} = \text{LAST}(\text{LIST}(A(N_i)))$.

In order to compute the production dependent graph, we use the iterating approach as shown in Fig. 5.1. In the figure, A_N denotes the node dependent array of node N. It is used to record the superposition effect on N.

Firstly, we assign the corresponding values to each dependent array A_p, according to the dependent graph $D(p)$, and set the superposition effects on each node N.

Now we may enter into the iterating body. For each production $p, p \in P$,

$$p : N_0 ::= N_1 \ldots N_{n_p}, \quad n_p \geq 0,$$

each node subarray $A_p(N_i)$, where $i \in [0..n_p]$, is dated, according to the node dependent array A_N, where $N = N_i$. Then the closure of the dependent array A_p is computed. Finally, according to each node subarray $A_p(N_i)$, where $i \in [0..n_p]$, the corresponding node dependent array A_N, where $N = N_i$, is dated.

After all production are processed in the way mentioned above, if we find that there is a node dependent array which is dated in this process, we enter into the iterating body again. We end this process when there is no such node dependent array.

In the algorithm for computing dependent graphs, for each production, the maximum number of attributes within a production is $|D|$. So there are

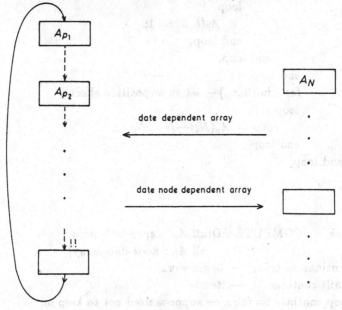

Fig. 5.1. The interating approach for computing production dependent graph.

at most $|D|^2$ values assigned in each A_p. The complexity of this algorithm is $O(|P||D|^2)$.

In the algorithm for computing production dependent graphs, the complexity of computing closure is $O(|D|^3)$, and the complexity of dating node subarrays and node dependent arrays is $O(|D|)$. Since $O(|D|^3)$ is much greater than $O(|D|)$, the complexity of while-loop executed once is $O(|P||D|^3)$. Whether a new iteration is needed depends on whether some node dependent array is dated in the last iteration. In the worst case, only one attribute in a node dependent array is dated in each iteration. Thus the while-loop is repeated at most $|V||X|^2$ times. So the complexity of this alogorithm is $O(|P||D|^3|V||X|^2)$.

procedure   COMPUTE-DEPENDENT-GR(all A_p: dependent-array,
                                            all A_n: node-dep-array);
begin   for every $p, p \in P$ — $p : N_0 ::= N_1 \ldots N_{n_p}$, $n_p \geq 0$
          loop $A_p := 0$;   — set initial values
                for every $F, F \in r_p$
                loop for every $\bar{a}, \bar{a} \in DS(F)$— compute dependent
                      loop for every $\bar{b}, \bar{b} \in US(F)$— graph

```
                    loop
                        A_p(\overline{b}, \overline{a}) := 1;
                    end loop;
                end loop;
            end loop;
        for i in (0..n_p)— set superposition effect
        loop
                A_N := A_p(N_i)—N = N_i
        end loop
    end loop;
end;
```

```
procedure      COMPUTE-PD(all A_p: dependent-array,
                                all A_N: node-dep-array);
begin continue := true;   — begin work
    while continue      — iterate
    loop continue := false; — suppose need not to keep on
        for every p, p ∈ P— process production p
        loop   — p : N_0 ::= N_1 ... N_{n_p}, n_p ≥ 0
            for i in (0..n_p) — date node subarray
            loop
                    A_p(N_i) := A_N;—N_i = N
            end loop
            A_p := A_p^+;      — compute closure
            for i in (0..n_p) — check node subarray
            loop
                if A_p(N_i) = A_n—N_i = N
                    then continue := true; — need to keep on
                        A_N := A_p(N_i); — date node
                                        — dependent array
                end if;
            end loop;
        end loop;
    end loop;
end;
```

In order to check whether there is a circle in a production dependent graph, what is to be done is to check whether there is '1' in the diagonal in a dependent array A_p. So the complexity of this algorithm is $O(|P||D|)$.

In fact, we deal with the attribute sequence table, the instruction sequence table and the driving sequence table as a whole. That is, whenever a production dependent array A_p is processed, the corresponding attribute sequence, instruction sequence, and driving sequence are computed. We use a one-dimensional array to implement the driving sequence table. Its index type is the integer type and the index denotes the state of the driving sequence table. Its component subtype is the sequence type and the component is used to specifiy the driving sequence.

The algorithm for computing attribute sequence is to order the attributes in a dependent array A_p according to some conditions. So, its complexity is $O(|D|^2)$.

The driving sequence of a production may be transferred directly from its attribute sequence. So, the complexity for computing driving sequence is $O(|D|)$.

Since $O(|D|^2)$ is much greater than $O(|D|)$, the complexity of computing driving sequence table is $O(|P||D|^2)$.

```
procedure   CHECK-CIRCLE(all A_p: dependent-array,
                                circle: boolean);
begin   circle := false;      — suppose no circle
        ch: for every p, p ∈ P
            loop for every ā, ā ∈ A(p) — check circle
                loop if A_p(ā, ā) = 1
                    then
                            circle := true; — has circle
                            exit ch;
                    end if;
                end loop;
            end loop;
end;
```

```
procedure   CREAT-DVT(all A_p: dependent-array,
                            DST: driving-array);
begin   state := 0;      — set initial state
        for every p, p ∈ P  — p : N_0 ::= N_1 ... N_{n_p}, n_p ≥ 0
```

```
        loop COMPUTE-AS(A_p, L); — compute attribute sequence
              COMPUTE-DV(DST, L, state);
                                        — compute driving sequence
        end loop;
end;



procedure   COMPUTE-AS(A_p: dependent-array, L: att-seq);
begin L := ( );                              — initialize sequence
      choice:= "inherited attribute";   — attribute kind
      while A(p) ≠ SET(L)              — order attribute
      loop for every ā, ā ∈ A(p) and ā ∉ SET(L)
            loop if ā is choice          — check kind
                        then success := true; – suppose condition hold
                        ch: for every b̄, b̄ ∈ A(p)
                            loop if A_p(b̄, ā) = 1 and b̄ ∉ SET(L)
                                    then success := false;
                                            exit ch; — fail to hold
                                  end if;
                            end loop;
                        if success    — condition hold
                            then L := L ∘ (ā);
                            end if;
                  end if;
            end loop;
            if choice = "inherited attribute"    — change kind
              then choice := "synthesized attribute"
              else choice := "inherited attribute"
            end if;
      end loop;
end;



procedure   COMPUTE-DV(DST: driving-array, L: att-seq,
                              state: integer);
begin while L ≠ ( )
      loop state := state +1;  — set new state
            DST(state) := ( );  — initialize sequence
```

```
    on: loop
          case FIRST(L) of
          when a̅, a̅ ∈ S(N₀) → DST(state):= DST(state)
                                          ∘(F_val);
                              -∃F ∈ r_p,  a̅ ∈ DS(F)
                          L := REST(L);
          when a̅, a̅ ∈ I(N₀) → L := REST(L);
                              if ∃b̅ ∈ A(p),  A_p(b̅, a̅) = 1
                              then
                                  DST(state):=
                                  DST(state)∘(↑);
                                  exit on;
                              end if;
          when a̅, a̅ ∈ A(N_i),  N_i ∈ V_t,  i ∈ [1..n_p]
                          → L := REST(L);
          when a̅, a̅ ∈ I(N_i),  N_i ∈ V_n,  i ∈ [1..n_p]
                          → L := REST(L);
                              DST(state):=
                              DST(state)∘(F_val);
                              —∃F ∈ r_p,  a̅ ∈ DS(F)
          when a̅, a̅ ∈ S(N_i),  N_i ∈ V_n,  i ∈ [1..n_p]
                          → L := REST(L);
                              DST(state) ::=
                              DST(state) ∘(↓_{N_i});
                              exit on;
          when ∧        → exit on;
          end loop;
          DST(state):= DST(state) ∘(↑));
    end loop;
end;
```

The complexity of the whole algorithm for checking DAG and computing operation sequences is given by the following sum:

$$O(|P||D|^3|V||X|^2) + O(|P||D|) + O(|P||D|^2)$$
$$= O(|P||D|^3|V||X|^2)$$
$$= O(|X|^5|G||R|^2|V|).$$

From the sum above, we find that the complexity of the whole algorithm is linear. Here the most significant item is $|X|$. $|X|$ is the maximum number of attributes associated with a node and is rather small for AGs defining programming languages. So, our algorithm is practical.

In order to present some features of DAG, we will compare DAG with OAG in the next section.

6. The Comparison between DAG and OAG

Both ordered attribute grammar and dependent attribute grammar are subclasses of AGs on the basis of order — the dependent relations among attributes. However, they pay attention to different points. OAG is mainly concerned with the direct or indirect relations among attributes associated with each node in AGs. It must use related productions as mediums to compute these dependent relations. DAG immediately deals with the direct or indirect relations among attributes associated with nodes in each production in AGs. So, DAG looks natural and reflects the characteristics of AGs. In fact, these dependent relations are formed from the dependent relations between the attributes which belongs to the using attribute occurrence set of a semantic rule F associated with a production, and the attributes which belong to the defining attribute occurrence set of semantic rule F. According to the definition of AGs, a semantic rule must be associated with some production. Therefore, by means of studying the direct and indirect dependent attributes associated with nodes in production, we can understand more clearly the semantic rules associated with this production. In OAG, an immediate issue is dispersed to each node in AGs and the researched object is indirectly reflected through the direct and indirect relations among the attributes associated with these nodes. However, the features in these scattering nodes do not completely embody the whole object. So, at last, these scattering nodes must be linked together by corresponding productions in OAG.

In OAG, the task of checking subclasses of AGs and the task of computing operation sequences are combined together. So, its expressing power is cut down due to this. In order to compute operation sequences, any attributes associated with a node must be ordered in OAG and the complete dependency relation in each node is introduced. As a result, the attributes among which there are originally no dependent relations at all have dependent relations and it increases the chance to have circles in the extended dependency relations in OAG. It has been proved that DAG contains OAG. Another advantage of dealing with the checking subclasses of AGs and the computing operation sequences in two steps in DAG is that when a given AG is found not to belong to DAG, the corresponding operation sequences are not computed at all.

In the aspect of complexity, two subclasses of AGs are linear. While the complexity of OAG is $O(|X|^4|G||R|^3)$ (Ref. 2), the complexity of DAG is $O(|X|^5|G||R|^2|V|)$. It seems that DAG is much more complex than OAG. However, in the data given in OAG, the complexity of computing closure is $O(|D|^2)$, not $O(|D|^3)$. A parallel algorithm may be used to compute the closure. If $O(|D|^3)$ is taken as the complexity of computing closure, then the complexity of OAG becomes $O(|X|^5|G||R|^4)$. So, the ratio of complexity of OAG to DAG is $|R|^2 : |V|$. $|R|$ is the maximum number of nodes in a production, while $|V|$ is the number of nodes in an AG. For AGs defining programming languages, $|V|$ is slightly greater than $|R|^2$. For example, in the attribute grammar written for Pascal, $|R| = 7, |V| = 64$. In general, the complexities of two subclasses of AGs are close to each other.

7. Conclusion

The dependent attribute grammar is a new attribute grammar class. The complexity of the algorithm is close to that of the algorithm for OAG. That is, it depends polynomially in time on the size of input AGs. The algorithm is easy to be perceived and reflects clearly the characteristics of AGs. The class of DAG is greater than that of OAG.

A semantic analyzer generator based on DAG has been built. An AG for Pascal has been experimented in the generator. The result is satisfactory.

References

1. G.V. Bochmann, " Semantic evaluation from left to right", CACM **19**, (1976) 55-62.
2. U. Kastens, "Ordered attribute grammars", *Acta Imformatica* **13**, 3 (1980) 229-256.
3. U. Kastens and E. Zimmerman, "GAG — A generator based on attributed grammar", Institute fur Informatik II, Universitaet Karlsruhe, Berich Nr. 14/80.
4. K. Kennedy and S.K. Warren, "Automatic generation of effcient evaluators for attribute grammars", *POPL* **3** (1976) 32-49.
5. K.-J. Räihä, "On attribute grammar and their use in a compiler writing system", Report A-1977-4, Department of Computer Science, University of Helsinki, Helsinki (1977).
6. K.-J. Räihä et al., "Revised report on the compiler writing system HLP78", Report A-1983-1, Department of Computer Science, University of Helsinki, Helsinki (1983).

FILE TRANSLATION

Lin Junhai
Department of Computer Engineering
Nanjing Aeronautical Institute

Abstract

"File Translation" had been investigated by many authors in the 70's. A variety of proposals on file translation were built for the various computer systems. However, the generality is elusive and has not been achieved yet.

This paper gives a theoretical analysis of the problem and a normal description in file translation is also presented. Furthermore a mathematical model is proposed and a fill-in-the-form approach is designed on the basis of this model. With this model, the file translators can be automatically generated.

Based on this approach, a translator between relation databases has been realized by the author.

1. Introduction

The basic function of a file translator is to transfer data stored in a certain format to another one without loss of any information. Database translation is one of the important topics in file translations. In the 1970's, many papers discussing file translation had been published. Because it is tedious and time consuming to develop the file translator for each different system, many investigators tried hard to develop a file translator which can be used for all systems. However, it is very difficult to achieve this goal for the reasons discussed later.

At that time, most of the discussions had been focussed on the hierarchical or network model of data and on their implementations on large or mini computers[1,2]. They cannot be used in relation model without major modifications. Since then, almost all of the new commercial products of database system have been implemented in relation model. Generally, file translator is provided in system utilities[4]. But all those previous works have not yet achieved the goal of complete generality. For a certain system, it is only possible to import a file stored in another system to the specified system or to do it in reverse direction.

File translators can be classified into three categories according to the hierarchy of systems, which are the translators of operating system level, database system level (called database translation) and application level. In general, it is simple to translate a file in an operating system level into another file. The reason is obvious, because among the syntax and semantics of data in a file, only syntax is involved in file translation. One example is reading an IBM DOS file and writing it to a UNIX file[5]. Only the syntax of data in file is concerned. However one has to bear in mind that the semantics of data can be important in course of database translation. The types of data and their relationship must be defined clearly, otherwise loss of information may occur and result in confusion.

In this paper, the file translation is discussed in database level. A mathematical model of file translator as well as a scheme of implementing file translator are also proposed.

2. Files and Definitions of Files

In this paper, a file is defined as a partially ordered set of data structures making up of an ordered set of components. The component is a set of continuous bytes or a structure. As discussed earlier in section 1, there are three levels of translations. To be more explicit, the semantics of data in a file could have different meanings in different levels. For example, an underlying table in relation database may be a binary file from the point of view of operating systems. But database system will treat it as a set of structured records which consists of a certain number of fields. Whereas a specific application may consider that file as a payroll document. Actually, it is interpreted with different semantics from each level.

Structures can be either the same or of different types in a file. The length of a structure can be fixed or varied. The structures in a file are

partially, not completely ordered. In other words, if structure A is prior to
structure B, and B prior to C, then we have A prior to C. But for any two
structures S1 and S2, they may or may not be in order. The components
of a structure are ordered completely.

There are many types of files existing in various systems. One may
create a variety of files in the future. Our definition of a file is sufficient for
describing the syntax of files.

In order to store a file in a certain physical medium, it is necessary to
have a set of rules for the purpose of locating each structure in the file.
A class of files stored in a medium can be defined completely by a partly
ordered set of data structures and a set of positioning rules. A specific
file will be produced by assigning values to each component of each data
structure in a file.

An example of file is shown below:

TABLE 0, 1 "PROFIT REPORT"		structure 1
VECTORS 0, 4 " "		structure 2
TUPLES 0, 3 " "		structure 3
LABEL 1, 0 "YEAR"		structure 4
LABEL 2, 0 "SALES"		structure 5
LABLE 3, 0 "COST"		structure 6
LABEL 4, 0 "PROFIT"		structure 7

DATA

0, 0   structure 8

" "

−1, 0

BOT

0, 1980

V

0, 100   structure 9

0, 90

V

0, 10

V

−1, 0

BOT

0, 1981

V

0, 110

V   structure 10

0, 101

V

0, 9

V

−1, 0

BOT

0, 1982

V

0, 121

V   structure 11

0, 110

V

0, 11

V

−1, 0

EDD

This is an underlying table in relation database called "PROFIT REPORT"
and consists of 11 structures, which belong to six types of structures individ-
ually. Type 1 includes structure 1, which contains relation name "PROFIT

REPORT". Type 2 has structure 2, which stipulates the number of fields in each record. Digit 4 in the second component of this structure points out that there are 4 fields in each record. Type 3 involves the structure 3, which declares that the number of records in table is 3. Type 4 includes four structures namely 4, 5, 6 and 7. Each of them tells a name of fields. Type 5 has the structure 8, which indicates that data will appear in the following structures. Type 6 includes structures 9, 10 and 11, which are the values of three records.

3. The Translation of Files

The data stored in a database usually are organized as files. Therefore database translation is one of the problems of file translation. As mentioned above, a class of files is specified by a partially ordered set of structures and a set of positioning rules. The translation of files can be defined as a map M:

$$F = M(f)$$

where f is a source file belonging to a certain class of files, F is the target file (the map of file f). Usually map file F and source file f belong to different classes of files. A constraint on map M is required, that is any piece of information derived from file f can also be derived from map file F.

The problem to be solved in mapping is how to figure out the value of each component of structures in target file in accordance to the definitions of files (source and target) discussed in section 2. In fact, we have to compose a set of formulae and assignment commands to evaluate variables of target files.

4. A Mathematical Model of File Translator

Before discussion of implementing file translators, we give a mathematical model of translator as follows[3]:

⟨⟨convertor⟩⟩::= begins ⟨files⟩ ends begint ⟨files⟩ endt
⟨files⟩::= ⟨f_head⟩⟨ structs⟩⟨order⟩
⟨f_head⟩::= ⟨f_from⟩⟨ f_type⟩⟨delimiter⟩
⟨f_from⟩::= entry | *.⟨exten⟩ | ⟨batch⟩
⟨exten⟩::= ⟨string⟩
⟨batch⟩::= ⟨batch_name⟩.bch
⟨batch_name⟩::= ⟨string⟩
⟨f_type⟩::= A | a | B | b

⟨delimiter⟩::= null | ⟨string⟩

⟨structs⟩::= ⟨struct⟩ | ⟨struct⟩⟨structs⟩
⟨struct⟩::= ⟨s_head⟩⟨components⟩
⟨s_head⟩::= ⟨s_name⟩⟨num_component⟩
⟨s_name⟩::= ⟨string⟩
⟨num_component⟩::= ⟨integer⟩
⟨components⟩::= ⟨component⟩ | ⟨component⟩⟨components⟩

⟨component⟩::= ⟨c_name⟩⟨c_type⟩⟨c_from⟩ ⟨coding⟩⟨size⟩⟨formula⟩⟨ value⟩
                    | ⟨struct⟩
⟨c_name⟩::= ⟨string⟩
⟨c_type⟩::= ⟨C⟩ | ⟨V⟩ | ⟨S⟩
⟨C⟩::= C | c
⟨V⟩::= V | v
⟨S⟩::= S | s
⟨c_from⟩::= calculate | entry | null
⟨coding⟩::= A | a | B | b| null
⟨size⟩::= ⟨integer⟩
⟨formula⟩::= ⟨exp⟩
⟨value⟩::= null | ⟨exp⟩
⟨order⟩::= ⟨s_name⟩ [, s_name]

Symbols which are not in ⟨ ⟩ indicate terminals. Here terminal "begins"
is a reserved word, which indicates the beginning of source file. "ends"
indicates the end of source file. "begint" means the beginning of target file
and "endt", the end of target file. Terminal "entry" means entered by user,
and "A", ASCII; "B", binary; "C", constant; "V", variable and "S", string.
Null means unknown. ⟨Formula⟩ is a mapping function which stipulates
how to calculate the value of component in a structure in target file from
source file. ⟨String⟩, ⟨integer⟩ and ⟨exp⟩ are the definitions of character
string, integer and expression respectively. We omit them here.

5. Implementation

There may be two ways to implement the translator of files: "programming" and "fill-in-the-form". In programming, user needs to know a new
language of translation. But once a translator is generated by using the
language, user no longer needs this language, if he or she does not want
to have a new translator of files. That means user is required to learn a
language which is seldom used.

We propose a fill-in-the-form approach instead of a language. A few forms are created and shown on the screen one by one. The simple work user has to do is to fill data in the forms according to the instructions which are displayed on the screen. The system will generate the translator of files needed.

It is helpful to note the following facts when one creates the forms for generating the translator of files.

Data stored in files can be classified into two categories: the description of data and data themselves. The location of data descriptions is different from file to file. Four cases should be considered:

(1) *Simple File*

Data and their descriptions are located in separate areas in file, such as dBaseII and dBaseIII files. Data descriptions are stored in the head of file and followed by data.

(2) *Mixed File*

Data and their descriptions are included in the same file but cannot be separated into data description area and data area, such as Spread Sheet of Lotus 123.

(3) *Complex File*

Data and their descriptions are stored in different files such as XDB database system[4].

(4) *Default file*

Only data are contained in the file, the data descriptions are defined by default.

One may change some information such as changing field type, field name etc. in the translation of databases. In other words, the increasing or decreasing of information will happen although the regulation of no loss of information is violated.

6. Summary

By using this model and approach, the author has created a database translator which can translate several well-known files of databases such as dBaseII, dBaseIII, Lotus 123 and so forth into XDB database system[4]. This has worked for years. As we mentioned in section 5, no need of knowing a new language and ease of operator are the advantages of fill-in-the-form approach.

During the translation of a mixed file, the translator needs to scan the whole source file for several passes because the data descriptions are scattered anywhere in mixed files. For example, at first pass, translator figures out the number of fields and types of fields and then in the second pass transfers data from source to target. If the source file is very large, the efficiency of translation will drop down fast. The further work we need to do seems to be the optimization of the translators.

References

1. Edward W. Burss, James P. Fry "Generalized software for translating data", National Computer Conference, U.S.A., 1976.
2. N.C. Shu, B.C. Housel, V.Y. Lum, "CONVERT: A high level translation definition language for data conversion", *Communications of ACM* **18**, Oct. 1975.
3. D. Gries, *Compiler Construction for Digital Computers*, 1971.
4. *XDB User's Manual*, Software System Technology, Inc., U.S.A., 1986.
5. *UNIX System V Programmer's Manual*, AT&T, 1985.

IMPROVEMENTS IN JACKSON'S PROGRAM
INVERSION TECHNIQUES

Xu Yongsen & He Biao
Department of Computer Science
Nanjing University

Abstract

In Michael Jackson's Program Design Method, the most important part is the resolution of structure clash using program inversion techniques.

This paper makes some improvements in the program inversion techniques, which exploit the limit of the use of loop statements in the inverted program. Having extended Jackson's structure diagram to express the recursive structures, this paper also illustrates how to use the improved techniques to resolve the recursive problems.

1. Introduction

Michael Jackson shows that the input and output data of a program can be expressed by the consistent and logical hierarchical structures (structure diagram), and the structure of the program must be based on the structures of all data. The program can be developed from its inherent data structures, if 1–1 correspondence exist between them[1,2].

A problem occurs when the necessary 1–1 correspondence cannot be found, and a program has to process two or more conflicting structures. Jackson defines this as a structure clash, and demonstrates a method involving "Program Inversion" to solve the clash.

The program inversion techniques given by Jackson limits the structure of inverted programs, and lead to a strong demand to avoid using loop statements in the inverted program, instead use a lot of goto statements. Thus, the programs are neither readable nor understandable.

Clarity and simplicity are criteria of programming[3,4]. This paper makes some improvements in the return control mechanism of program inversion techniques. The program inverted by the improved techniques will have a well structured style.

Jackson's structure diagram is unable to express recursive structures. This paper attempts to extend the structure diagram to do so. Together with the use of the improved program inversion techniques, non-recursive program can be developed to solve the recursive problems. The proof of mathematical property of the extended structure diagram will be left till another paper.

Like Jackson's indication, our ideas are also illustrated through some examples. The programs given are written in PASCAL or PASCAL-like language.

2. The Refinements of Return Control Mechanism in the Program Inversion

Program inversion techniques are fully indicated in the discussion of the "TELEGRAMS ANALYSIS" problem[1]. Here we will introduce the program inversion briefly and indicate our improvement also by the processing of this problem.

At first, we quote the problem description as posed by Jackson:

Problem   "TELEGRAMS ANALYSIS"

An input file on tape contains the texts of a number of telegrams. The tape is accessed by a "read block" instruction, which read into main storage a variable-length character string delimited by a terminal EOB character: the size of a block cannot exceed 100 characters, excluding the EOB. Each block contains a number of words, separated by space characters; there may be one or more spaces between adjacent words, and at the beginning and the end of a block there may (but need not) be one or more additional spaces. Each telegram consists of a number of words followed by the special word "zzzz"; the file is terminated by a special end-file block, whose first character is EOF. In addition, there is always a null telegram at the end of the file, in the block preceding the special end-file block: this null telegram consists only the word "zzzz". Except for the fact that the null telegram always appears at the end of the file, there is no particular relationship between blocks and telegrams: a telegram may begin and end anywhere within a block, and may span several blocks; several telegrams may share a block.

The processing required is an analysis of the telegrams. A report is to be produced showing, for each telegram, the number of words it contains and the number of those words which are oversize (more than 12 characters). For the purpose of the report, "zzzz" does not count as a word, nor does the null telegram count as a telegram. The format of the report is:

TELEGRAMS ANALYSIS

TELEGRAM 1

   15 WORDS OF WHICH 2 OVERSIZE

TELEGRAM 2

   106 WORDS OF WHICH 13 OVERSIZE

TELEGRAM 3

   42 WORDS OF WHICH 0 OVERSIZE

...

END ANALYSIS

No attention need to be paid to the provision of page heading, skipping or the perforations in the paper, or other details of page formatting.

The data structure of the printed report is:

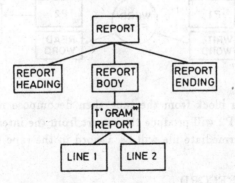

The data structure of the input tape is:

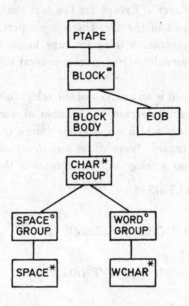

There is a clash between block and telegram report. The component "process block" and the component "process telegram" cannot both appear in one program structure, we need at least two.

We will restructure the system as:

P1 will read a block from the tape then decompose it and create an intermediate file; P2 will produce the report from the intermediate file. A record of the intermediate file will be a word in the tape file, this format will then be:

WORD=RECORD

        CCT: integer; {the length counter of the word}

WCH: packed array[1..100] of char; {the word body}

END

The structure of the intermediate file, as seen by P1, is:

The structure of the same file, as seen by P2, is:

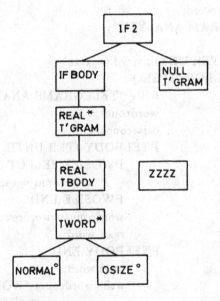

Schematic logic for P1 is:

```
P1   SEQ
       open ptape; open IF2;
       read block;
       PBODY ITER UNTIL eof-ptape
              BS:= 1; {character counter of block}
              PBLOCKBODY ITER UNTIL EOB
                     PCHARGROUP SELECT word
                                          build word;
                                          write word;
```

```
                PCHARGROUP OR          spacegroup
                                       process space;
                PCHARGROUP END
          PBLOCKBODY END
      PBODY END
      close IF1; close ptape;
P1    END
```

Schematic logic for P2 is:

```
P2    SEQ
      open IF2; read word;
      write "TELEGRAM ANALYSIS";
      telno:=1;
      PRPTBODY ITER UNTIL word = 'zzzz'
                PTELEGRAM SEQ
                        write "TELEGRAMS ANALYSIS";
                        wordcount:= 0;
                        osizecount:=0;
                        PTELBODY ITER UNTIL world = 'zzzz'
                            PWOSIZE SELECT cct> 12
                                osizecount:= osizecount + 1;
                            PWOSIZE END
                            wordcount:=wordcount + 1;
                            read word;
                        PTELBODY END
                        read word;
                        write wordcount "WORDS OF WHICH"
                                osizecount "OVERSIZE";
                PTELEGRAM END
                        telno:=telno + 1;
      PTELBODY END
      write "END ANALYSIS"
      read word;
      close IF2;
P2    END
```

Note the final "read word" statement: it reads one record beyond the "zzzz" of the null telegram, thus reading the EOF marker in the word file.

The first of the two structures fits the structure of the tape file; the second fits the structure of the report. The problem is reduced to simple processing of structures between which satisfactory 1–1 correspondence exist. So the clash is resolved.

But the inefficiency is inconvenient and sometimes intolerable. To be more efficient, we convert P1 or P2 so that it can run as a subroutine or procedure of the other. The conversion process is called program inversion.

If we choose to invert P2 with respect to word file, we will code it in such a manner that it can be used as a replacement for the "write word" procedure of P1. We then have:

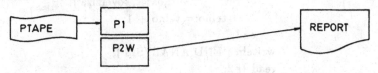

When P1 is required to write a word to the word file, it invokes P2W; P2W then disposes of the word, using it to contribute to the report, and return to P1. Provided that P1 writes all the words of the word file, its successive invocation of P2W will cause P2W to produce the complete report.

Alternatively, we can choose to invert P1 with respect to the word file, which could be used as a replacement for the "read word" procedure of P2. It will be of the same effect as inverting P2.

We will choose to invert P2, thus creating P2W.

The program coding can be directly derived from schematic logic. Here is PASCAL coding for P2:

```
PROGRAM P2(IF2, OUTPUT);
        TYPE WORD=RECORD
                    cct: integer;
                    wch: packed array[1 . . 100] of char;
                END;
        VAR  IF2:FILE OF WORD;
             telno. oszct, wrdct: integer;
        BEGIN
             open IF2; read IF2;
             writeln ('TELEGRAM ANALYSIS');
             telno:=1;
             with IF2!.  do
             while wch⟨⟩ 'zzzz' or cct⟨⟩4 do
                 begin
```

```
                              writeln (TELEGRAM', telno);
                              wrdct:=0;  oszct:=0;
                              while wch⟨⟩ 'zzzz' or cct⟨⟩ 4 DO
                              begin
                                    if cct > 12 then oszct:=oszct + 1:
                                    wrdct:=wrdct + 1;
                                    read IF2;
                              end;
                              read IF2;
                              writeln (wrdct, 'WORDS OF WHICH'
                                            ,oszct, 'oversize');
                              telno:= telno + 1;
                        end;
                  writeln ('END ANALYSIS');
                  read IF2;
                  close IF2;
      END.
```

Now we invert P2 with respect to the word file, to create a replacement for the "write word" procedure of P1. When P1 produces a word, it invokes P2W by the procedure-call

$$P2W(x) \quad \{\text{the type of x is word}\}$$

passing on each invocation the next word to be processed. The first call of P2W passes the word which is read by the "READ IF2" statement immediately following the "OPEN IF2" in P2; the last call passes the zzzz word of the null telegram.

The changes needed in P2 to convert into P2W are:

(1) Specify P2W as a procedure with one parameter whose type is a record of intermediate file;

(2) Remove the OPEN and CLOSE commands for IF2;

(3) Recode the READ statement to reflect the fact that P2W acquires records by returning to P1 and being invoked again.

READ statement of P2 will be replaced by coding which will have the effect:

return to P1 to acquire another record; resume operation of
P2W at the point immediately following the replaced "READ".

On the first invocation of P2W, we must begin execution at the point following the first READ statement in P2; the last READ statement in P2 causes the end-of-file marker to be read. P2W returns to P1 to read the EOF marker, but P1 will never invoke P2W again. Since P2 and P2W can both be directly derived from the schematic logic, there should be a good correspondence between them. The function of P2W is to process one word record passed by P1. P2W is required to do REPORT HEADING PRODUCTION, TELEGRAM HEADING PRODUCTION, TELEGRAM BODY, TELEGRAM ENDING PRODUCTION and REPORT ENDING PRODUCTION respectively according to different word type. Thus, when P1 invokes P2W again after P2W has returned to P1, the operation of P2W will be resumed at the appropriate point according to the type of word.

In Jackson's program inversion, the parts of the return link address and the procedure returning controller are all played by the "state variable" of the inverted program. We will use the integer variable QS as the "state variable" of P2W in this problem. It records the state of the process which P2W is concerned with, that is the point reached in the input word file and the point reached in producing the output record. When the value of QS is changed, P2W returns: when invoked again, a CASE statement in P2W will ensure that the execution resumes at the point specified by the link. This mechanism is equivalent to the normal subroutine linkage mechanism. Its effect is:

(1) Move n to QS. Remember the return address.

(2) Return. Transfer controls to P1, which will provide the service required.

(3) CASE QS OF..., picks up the return link and resumes execution at the point specified.

(4) 1,2,..., the labels of the various return addresses.

When there are LOOP statements in the program to be inverted, problems will occur. Actually, the LOOP statement sets a return link in its exit part to ensure that control can return correctly to its condition test part. READ statement may be included in the loop, so if the LOOP statement also appears in the inverted program, the procedure may return in the middle of the loop. But compiler does not guarantee that the loop return link will survive during the execution of procedure return.

Jackson suggested that the LOOP statement should be avoided in the inverted program, replaced by a lot of GOTO statements.

We have made some improvements in the program techniques, especially in return control mechanism. The problem involving LOOP statements is solved perfectly, GOTO statements are not used, and the inverted program will have a good correspondence with the original program.

Our ideas are:

(1) The exchange of the "state variable" does not stand for procedure return, but only stands for that the control of the inverted program should be transferred to the part which corresponds to the current state.

(2) Whether the procedure should return after it has done some work is controlled by a local boolean variable, such as the rptb which we will use in the "TELEGRAMS ANALYSIS" problem. It will be assigned value 'true' once it enters the inverted program. If it reserves true, the procedure does not return, the control will transfer to the point specified by the "state variable"; if it is changed to false, the procedure returns, and the "state variable" is reserved as return link address. When the procedure is invoked again, the execution will be resumed at the point specified by the link.

(3) The condition test part of a loop statement in original program must correspond to a "state" – a case label of the CASE statement in the inverted program. The part of loop return link is now also played by the state variable, the reexecution of loop depends on that the state variable has been changed to the value corresponding to the condition test part. There will be a invisible loop in the inverted program.

(4) Since loop can be nested, the case body of a case label in the inverted program could not completely correspond to a loop. How to enter the inner loop from the outer part will depend on proper exchange of case label (the value of state variable).

The type of declaration of word needed in P1 is just the same as in P2. QS must be specified as a global variable which will be assigned value 1 before the first invocation of P2W.

Here is PASCAL coding for P2W:

```
PROCEDURE P2W (X: WORD);
          VAR rptb: boolean;
              telno, wrdct, oszct: integer;
          BEGIN
              rtpb:=true;
              with x do
              while rptb do
              case QS of
          1:  begin
                  writeln ('TELEGRAMS ANALYSIS');
                  telno:=1;  QS:=2;
```

```
                    end;
            2:  if wch⟨⟩ 'zzzz' or cct⟨⟩4
                then begin
                            writeln ('TELEGRAM', ,telno);
                            wrdct:=0; oszct:=0;
                            QS:=3;
                    end
                else  QS:=5;
            3:  if wch⟨⟩ 'zzzz' or cct⟨⟩4
                then begin
                            if cct>12 then oszct:=oszct + 1;
                            wrdct:=wrdct + 1;
                            QS:=3; rptb:=false;
                    end
                else begin
                            QS:=4; rptb:=false;
                    end;
            4:  begin
                    writeln (wrdct, 'WORDS OF WHICH',
                            oszct, 'OVERSIZE');
                    telno:=telno + 1;
                    QS:=2; rptb:=false;
                end;
            5:  begin
                    writeln ('END ANALYSIS');
                    rptb:=false; RPTA:=false;
                end;
            end;
    END;
```

RPTA is a global boolean variable which must be assigned value 'true' before the first invocation of P2W. When it is true, the procedure need not be invoked again; when it is false, if the procedure is to be invoked, the input data must be invalid.

3. The Processing of Recursive Problem

Jackson's structure diagram is unable to express recursive structures. The structure diagram could be treated as a tree: the nodes of the tree are the components in the diagram; one component is part of another means that the node it corresponds to is the son of the node which corresponds to the other component. Jackson only use the tree in non-recursive form. That is to say, the leaves of the tree must be the basic components, and the nodes which are not leaves must be composite components.

Here we make some extension to it to express recursive structures:

A leaf of a subtree could be not only the basic component; but also the composite component whose corresponding node belongs to another subtree, or the ascendants of itself in this subtree or the whole tree. Thus, the extended diagram can well express recursive structures. The recursive tree has been proved reasonable. The proof that Jackson's Program Design Method can also use recursive diagram to develop recursive programs will be left till another paper. When writing schematic logic from the structure diagram, we may simply treat the component in the program structure which corresponds to the leaf we have just described as a procedure-call ("do component"). By using the improved program inversion techniques, we can develop the program in non-recursive form to solve the recursive problem from the program structure expressing it.

Consider this problem:

There is a simple language, the syntax of its arithmetic expression in BNF is:

⟨exp⟩   ::= ⟨term⟩|⟨addop⟩⟨term⟩|⟨exp⟩⟨addop⟩⟨term⟩
⟨term⟩   ::= ⟨factor⟩|⟨term⟩⟨mulop⟩⟨factor⟩
⟨factor⟩   ::= ⟨primary⟩|⟨factor⟩⟨exponenop⟩⟨primary⟩
⟨primary⟩   ::= ⟨pure number⟩|⟨variable⟩|(⟨exp⟩)
⟨addop⟩   ::= +|−
⟨mulop⟩   ::= *|/
⟨exponenop⟩ ::= ↑

The above definition could also be simply written as:

$$⟨exp⟩ ::= [⟨addop⟩] ⟨primary⟩\{⟨op⟩⟨primary⟩\}$$

An input file on tape contains the text of an expression. The tape is accessed by a "read block" instruction, which reads into main storage a invariable-length symbol string. Operators are treated as symbols, and the numbers and variables in the expression have already been transformed into symbols. The expression ends with special symbol "%". There are no more symbol beyond the "%", except for the end-of-file marker "EOF".

Now we wish to write a program to translate the input expression into a machine instruction sequence (a part of compiler). Here we only discuss the general processing principle, the details of producing instruction and some condition judgements are abbreviated.

Data structures of input and output are:

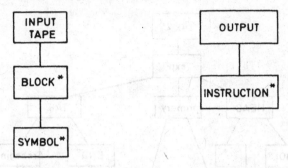

Since INSTRUCTION cannot be derived from BLOCK, they do not correspond, so there is a structure clash.

To solve the clash using program inversion, we still need to introduce an intermediate file and two programs – P1 and P2. Each recorded in the intermediate file will be symbol in the input file. P1 reads a block from the input file, decomposes it, and writes the symbol into the symbol file. P2 then produce the instructions according to the symbol read from the symbol.

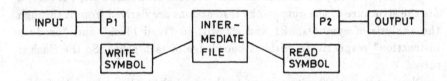

The structure of the symbol file, as seen by P1, is:

The structure of the same file, as seen by P2, is:

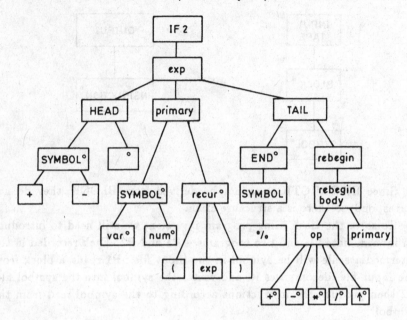

The first of these structures fits the structure of the tape file; the second fits the structure of the output—the instructions are derived from it through the analysis of symbols. P1 and P2 will do "read block" and "produce instruction" respectively, without knowledge of each other. So the clash is solved.

Now we invert P2 with respect to the symbol file, to replace the "write symbol" procedure in P1; thus creating P2W.

When P1 produces a symbol, it invokes P2W, passing on that symbol; P2W then does some work according to that symbol and returns to P1 to acquire another symbol. The program structure of P2 is just the same as that of data structure, only add "process" before the component name; the instruction production is seen as an elementary operation in it.

We can define the elementary operation available according to the recursive decent compiling techniques[5,6].

The schematic logic for P2 is:

```
P2   SEQ
     read symbol;
     PEXP SEQ
          i:=i + 1;   w[i]:= '$';
```

```
PHEAD      SELECT symbol='–'
           i:=i + 1; w[i]:= '–'; read symbol;
PHEAD      OR symbol='+'
           read  symbol;
PHEAD      END
PPRIMARY SELECT symbol='num'
           j:= j + 1; op[j]:=symbol; read symbol;
PPRIMARY OR        symbol='var'
           j:= j + 1; op[j]:=symbol; read symbol;
PPRIMARY OR        symbol
           read symbol; DO PEXP; read symbol;
           PTEST SELECT symbol ⟨ ⟩')'
                 ERROR;
           PTEST OR        symbol=')'
                 read symbol;
           PTEST END
PPRIMARY END
PTAIL      SELECT     symbol='operator'
           PX ITER UNTIL symbol ='%'
                     PREBEGIN SELECT   w[i]='$'
                              i:= i + 1; w[i]:=symbol;
                              read   symbol;
                              DO PPRIMARY;
                     PREBEGIN OR "The priority of
                              element on the top
                              of stack w is higher than
                              that of the symbol."
                              i:= i + 1; w[i]:= symbol;
                              read symbol;
                              DO PPRIMARY;
                     PREBEGIN END
                     PPRODUCE SEQ
                              "Producing the
                              instruction according
                              to the elements
                              on the top of
                              stack w and opa.";
                              i := i – 1;
                              j := j – 1 or  (according to
```

```
                                        j := j - 2; the unary or
                                                     binary operator.)
                                        j := j + 1;
                                        opa[j] := 'ac';
                                                     (Accumulator)
                                        DO ptail;
                        PPRODUCE END
            PX END
PTAIL       OR        symbol = '%'
            PY        SELECT w[i] ⟨ ⟩'$'
                      DO PRIMARY;
            PY        END
            i:=i−1;
PTAIL       END
PEXP END
P2  END
```

W is the stack to store operators; while opa is the stack to store oprands. Since the structure is recursive, and the operators must be compared in the same level of recursion; as soon as the component "do pexp" begins, a "level separator" '$' must be put into the stack w.

Note that some "do component" in schematic logic are only the needed available operations, which could be seen as procedure-call.

Using the improved program inversion techniques, we can get a PASCAL-like coding for P2W.

Here we omit the schematic and program coding for P1, which is very obvious.

The necessary declaration in P1 are:

TYPE SYMBOL: ......
VAR w, opa:array [1..10000] of symbol; (or bigger)
    QS, i, j: integer;
    rptb: boolean;

QS and rpta are of the same effect as those we have used in "TELE-GRAMS ANALYSIS" problem. Before the first invocation of P2W, QS, rpta, i and j will be assigned value 1, true, 0 and 0 respectively.

The procedure specification of P2W is:

```
PROCEDURE P2W (x: symbol);
        VAR    rptb: boolena;
        BEGIN
            rptb:=true;
            while rptb do
            case QS of
            1: begin
                    i:=i + 1; w[i]:= '$';
                    QS:=2;
                end;
            2: if x='-' then begin
                            i:=i + 1; w[i]:= '-';
                            QS:=4; rptb:=false;
                        end
                    else   QS:=3;
            3: if x='+' then begin
                            QS:=4; rptb:=false;
                        end
                    else   QS:=4;
            4: if x='(' then begin
                            QS:=1; rptb:=false;
                        end
                    else QS:=5;
            5: if x='num' or x='var'
                    then begin
                            j:=j + 1; opa[j]:=x;
                            QS:=6; rptb:=false;
                        end
                    else   error
            6: if x='operator,
                    then begin
                            if w[i]='$'
                            then begin
                                    i:=i+1;
                                    w[i]:=x;
                                    rptb:=false;
                                    QS:=4;
```

```
                                          end
                              else if "The priority
                                       of element on
                                       the top of
                                       stack w is
                                       less than
                                       that of x"
                                   then begin
                                          i:=i+1;
                                          w[i]:=x;
                                          QS:=4;
                                          rptb:=false;
                                          end
                                   else QS:=7
                      end
             else if x⟨ ⟩ '%' or x⟨ ⟩')'
                   then error
                   else QS:=8;
    7: begin

             "Producing the object instruction
              according to the elements on the top
              of stack w and opa";
              i:=i-1;
              j:=j-1 or (according to unary or
              j:=j-2;       binary operator)
              j:=j+1;
              opa[j]:='ac'; (accumulator)
              QS:=6;

       end;
    8: if x=')' then begin
                      QS:=6; rptb:=false;
                      end
             else if w[i]='$'
                   then begin
                          i:=i-1;
                          RPTA:=false;
                          rptb:=false;
                          end
                   else QS:=7;
```

```
                        end;
END;
```

This is a non-recursive program, it is equivalent to a recursive one. The procedure-call in inverted program is replaced by the proper exchange of state variable. Its function is like a recursive decent syntax analyzer of expression transformed into the symbol.

4. Conclusion

This paper has attempted to show how the Jackson's program inversion techniques can be improved by the refinements of return control mechanism, and how the extension to structure diagram can be made. Through some examples, it is shown that the limit to use loop statement in the inverted program is released, and recursive problem can be solved without involving recursive program structure by combining the improved inversion techniques with the extended structure diagram. Well structured program can be developed accurately and more conveniently.

We believe that along with the continuous consummation of itself, Jackson's Program Design Method will be successfully applied not only in data processing field, but also in a lot of other fields of computer science and technology.

References

1. M.A. Jackson, *Principle of Program Design*, Academic Press, 1975.
2. M.A. Jackson, *System Development*, Prentice-Hall, 1983.
3. N. Wirth, "On the design of programming languages", *Proc. IFIP Congress* **74** (1974) 386-393, North-Holland, Amsterdam.
4. Xu Jiafu, *System Programming Language*, Scientific Press, Beijing, 1983.
5. A.J.T. Daive and R. Morrison, *Recursive Descent Compiling*, Ellis Horwood Limited, England, 1981.
6. Zhen Guoliang and Xu Yongsen, *Compiling Methods*, Posts and Telecommunications Press, Beijing, 1982.
7. M. Stubbs, "An examination of the resolution of structure clashes by structure inversion", *The Computer Journal* **27**, No. 4 (1984).
8. O.J. Dahl, E.W. Dijkstra and C.A.R. Hoare, *Structured Programming*, Academic Press, 1972.
9. Ed Yourdon and L.L. Constantine, *Structured Design*, Yourdon Press, 1978.
10. A.D. Woodall, "Psycho-somatric structure clashes", *Computer Bulletin*, (June, 1982).

AN IMPLEMENTATION OF THE GRAPHICAL KERNEL SYSTEM (GKS)*

Xiong Yihua, Huang Zhizhong & Liu Shenquan
Institute of Computing Technology, Academia Sinica

Abstract

An implementation of Graphical Kernel System on a micro-computer is presented, special attention being paid to the workstations, segment and segment storage.

The language binding and the languages used in the implementation are also described.

1. Introduction

Graphical Kernel System (GKS), the first international standard for graphical systems, was specified by the West German in late 1970's. GKS defines two-dimensional standard and the 3-D extension can be added to it.

We have implemented this standard on a microcomputer with UNIX system. This implementation is at "2c" level.

---

*Project supported by the National Fund of Sciences.

73

2. Hardware

Hardware facilities include a microcomputer MC-68000 running UNIX, a color graphic display controller Model One/25, a video monitor with resolution 512 by 512, a local terminal, a digitizing tablet and a plotter. Figure 1 shows the configuration.

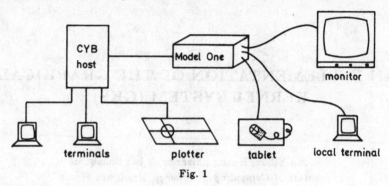

Fig. 1

3. Languages

GKS is language independent. Therefore, language binding is needed to provide an interface between GKS and the application program written in a specified language. The FORTRAN Binding is used in this implementation.

Since FORTRAN cannot support many useful functions such as automatic storage allocation and complex data structure, while assembly language limits portability, C language is used instead to implement most part of GKS. Assembly programs are needed to provide an interface between FORTRAN and C.

Therefore each GKS function programs are completed in one of the following three manners (Figure 2):

(1) all of the function program is in FORTRAN; the error handling functions are examples.

(2) all in C;

(3) most part in C and some part in FORTRAN.

4. Data Structure

The data structure is also implemented using C and FORTRAN. The C part of it corresponds to C programs and the FORTRAN part corresponds to FORTRAN programs.

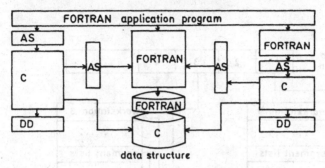

Note : AS - assembly interface ;   DD - device driver

Fig. 2

Most parts of the data structure, such as "GKS State List" and "Workstation State List", are implemented in C. A window in world coordinate (WC), for example, is defined as following:

```
typedef struct{
        float        x, y;
        }Wc;                        /* a WC point */


typedef struct{
                Wc      11, ur;
        }Window                     /* a window in WC */
```

A smaller part of the data structure as "Error File" is written in FORTRAN.

Figure 3 shows the relations between "Segment State List" and "Workstation State List".

5. Workstations

Seven workstations are supported. They are

(1) OUTIN: Model One, monitor and tablet;
(2) OUTPUT: plotter;
(3) WISS: Workstation Independent Segment Storage;
(4) (5), (6) & (7) MO or MI: metafiles

Here, the metafiles are implemented as UNIX files.

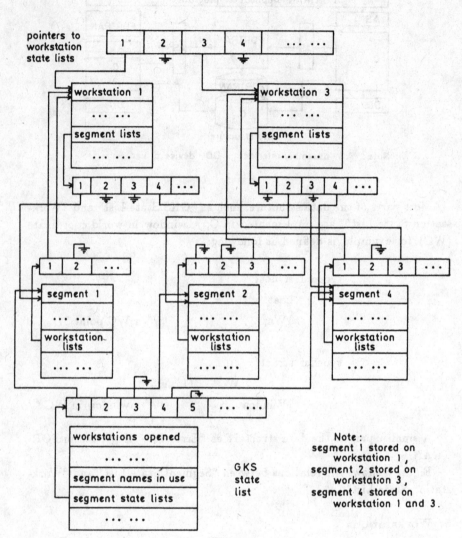

Fig. 3

6. Output

The six kinds of output primitives are all supported. The output procedure of polyline, for instance, is as follows:

```
PROCEDURE g_polyline (n, px, py);   {n: number of points}
BEGIN
            CASE w_ type OF
            normalized transformation;
            IF segment opened
                    THEN
                    BEGIN
                            segment storing;
                            segment transformation
                    END;
            w_polyline (n, px, py,...)
END;


PROCEDURE w_polyline (n, px, py,...);
BEGIN
            FOR w:=1 TO wk_max DO      {loop for every workstations}
                    BEGIN
                            IF (workstation w is OUTIN or OUTPUT)
                            AND w is active
                            THEN
                                    BEGIN
                                            clipping;
                                            workstation transfor-
                                                    mation;
                                            assigning attributes;
                                            d_polyline (n, px, py,...,
                                                    w, w_type)
                    END
END
PROCEDURE d_polyline (n, px, py,..., w, w_type);
BEGIN
            CASE w_type OF
                    1: d_1_polyline (n, px, py,..., w);
                    2: d_1_polyline (n, px, py,..., w);
                    3: ... ...
```

```
                        ... ...
                     k: ... ...
            END
END;
```

The program d_polyline( ) forms a thin cover which makes the difference between workstations unseen to the system so as to realise device independence. d_1_polyline performs polyline drawing on workstation of type 1.

With the adaptation to w_polyline( ), the segment redrawing procedure is implemented as follows:

```
PROCEDURE seg_redraw (seg_name);
BEGIN

        ... ...
        read an item from segment;
        CASE item type OF
              polyline:
                      BEGIN
                              segment transformation;
                              w_polyline (...)
                      END;
              ... ...
        END;
        ... ...
END;
```

7. Segment Storage

The two kinds of segment storage, WDSS and WISS, are implemented in the same manner. This produces the following advantages:

(1) dual storage of a segment is avoided;
(2) the transference from WISS to WDSS is simplified; and
(3) the segment manipulation is also simplified.

Each segment is stored in memory as a linked list of blocks of the same size (Figure 4).

The content of a segment consists of a sequence of items. An item can be:

(1) an output primitive;
(2) an output attribute, geometric or non-geometric;

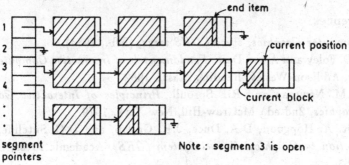

Note : segment 3 is open

Fig. 4

(3) a pick identifier;

(4) a clipping rectangle; or

(5) an end item indicating the end of the segment,

Figure 5 shows the procedure of drawing a segment into display.

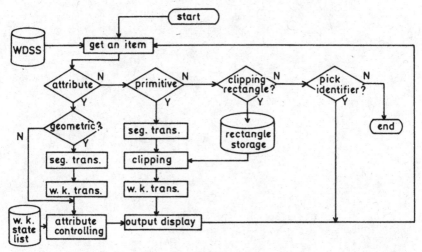

Fig. 5

8. Others

The input and interactive techniques, error handling, metafile output and input, etc., are all implemented according to the standard.

References

1. *Computer Graphics, special GKS issue*, (Feb., 1984).
2. J.D. Foley and A.van Dam, *Fundamentals of Interactive Computer Graphics*, Addison-Wesley, Reading Mass., 1982.
3. W.M. Newman and R.F Sproull, *Principles of Interactive Computer Graphics*, 2nd ed., McGraw-Hill, New York, 1979.
4. F.R. A. Hopgood, D.A. Duce, J.R. Gallop, and D.C. Sutcliffe, *Introduction to Graphical Kernel System (GKS)*, Academic Press, London, 1983.

THE PROCESS STRUCTURE OF DISTRIBUTED RELATIONAL DATABASE MANAGEMENT SYSTEM C-POREL

Chen Weimin*
Computer Science Dept.
Zhongshan Univ.

Zhou Longxiang
Inst. of Math.
Academia Sinica

Abstract

In this paper the Process Structure of Distributed Relational Database Management System C-POREL matching the features of UNOS operating system is described. The performance evaluation and the structure analysis are also given.

1. The Architecture of C-POREL

C-POREL is a unified Distributed Relational Database Management System established on the UV-68 microcomputers possessing the UNOS

---

*This is the work during visiting Inst. of Math. Academia Sinica.

81

operating system and connecting with the network of ETHERNET. Its designing target is to reach practicability, advancement, flexibility and limited portability. It is designed by Inst. of Math., Acad. Sinica and cooperated with the Shanghai Univ. of Science & Technology and East China Normal Univ.

According to Ref. 1, we now illustrate the principal logical structure of C-POREL. Fig. 1 gives the architecture of C-POREL system.

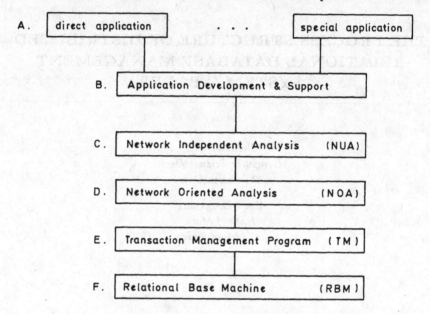

Fig. 1. The logical structure of C-POREL

A. The *Direct Application* and *Special Application* level is user oriented. In the *Direct Application* interface the user may specify interactively Relational Data Base Language (RDBL)[10] transactions or PASCAL-Relational Data Base Language (P-RDBL) transactions. In the *Special Application* interface, the user can select, combine, recombine and execute different prepared programs from an application library, these programs may be written in schematized P-RDBL.

B. The *Application Development & Support* level takes the P-RDBL transactions to precompile and guides the stand alone RDBL transactions into NUA.

C. The *Network Independent Analysis (NUA)* level translates the RDBL program into the Relational Machine Language (RML) form — The Language of RBM (see point F below). NUA does not have to know about the network or the distribution of relations and subrelations in the network. Meanwhile, NUA carries out the Integrity checking, Identification authentication and algebra optimization.

D. The *Network Oriented Analysis (NOA)* analyzes the RML transactions output from NUA. The NOA utilizes the knowledge about network configuration to split transactions into sub-transactions where each subtransaction can be executed on the signal node of the network. The distribution of these subtransactions is determined such that the processing cost and the data communication traffic between nodes will be minimized. The NOA also produces the necessary RML statements for subtransaction distribution and data transportation.

E. The *Transaction Management Program (TM)* manages execution of the transactions. It is in charge of the transaction scheduling, time ordering, resource request, communications, concurrency control, failure checking and recovery. Every node has exactly one TM. It is the most complex part of C-POREL system.

F. *The Relational Base Machine (RBM)* will be activated and managed by the TM for the execution of RML subtransactions. RBM processes the Relational Algebra Programs which are expressed via RML and by TM, evaluates assertions and checks consistency.

The relations of C-POREL are partitioned into horizontal fragmentations called subrelations. They may be distributed in different nodes. The system catalogs consists of long catalog and short catalog[5]. The short catalog contains the slowly changing schema description information such as relation schema, subrelation distribution tree, assertion and user identification. It preserves a uniform version in all network sites. The long catalog contains the information which is changing relatively frequently, e.g., the size of subrelation, the value distribution in its attribute, access path, etc. It is only kept at network sites where corresponding subrelation is actually stored.

The Communication System (CS) is in charge of all data and messages transmission among the network sites. It is different from POREL system — the data and messages transmission among the system modules of the local sites are accomplished by Inter-process Communication Mechanism of

Operating System (OS), not by the CS.

2. The Process Structure of C-POREL

2.1. *The disposition between DBMS and OS*

The design of multiuser DBMS is facing the problem of how to dispose the DBMS and OS. In general, there are two ways of disposition:

(1) DBMS is the extension of OS.

(2) DBMS is independent of OS.

The target of the first way is to remove the difference between DBMS and OS. Functions of DBMS are realized with the primitives of OS. Some functions such as the Storage Management, Process Scheduling, Data Recovery are really the tasks of OS, so this way of combining two into one is rather instructive[2]. The problem of "Double Pagging" in DBMS can also be resolved completely by this way, because the uncoordination between DBMS scheduling and OS scheduling may not happen. But the current OS is unable to bring the DBMS requirements into its own, so most of DBMS, e.g. System R, INGRES, POREL used the second way, so does the C-POREL system.

In the case of the second way, DBMS is independent of OS. Usually every concurrent DB user program runs in the separate process space. DBMS has to resolve the following problems:

- DBMS and User program are in the same process or not?
- DBMS actually runs with many processes or DBMS runs in only one process under multitasking way?
- How to realize concurrency control?
- How to coordinate between DBMS scheduling and OS scheduling?

For the second way, DBMS is the "Application Program" of OS and managed by OS, e.g. in System R, each concurrent user creates and runs a separate process, the buffer pool and lock table should be handled as shared segments of DBMSs, the concurrency control and coordination management are implemented through the shared segments, Fig. 2 shows this possibility. INGRES partially follows the structure mentioned above. Since UNIX has no shared data segments, INGRES must put lock table inside the OS and provides buffering private to each user. For this way, the shared segments should be the critical section. In general, we handle the completion of the critical section through setting and releasing the short-term locks which basically simulates the semaphores. A problem may arise if the OS scheduler deschedules a DB process which is holding such a lock. All other DB processes cannot execute continuously for very long without accessing the critical section. This will produce a devastative effect on performance[4].

C-POREL runs in UNOS operating system. UNOS is developed on MC 68000 microcomputer series and compatible with UNIX. UNOS extends message system from UNIX, which includes pipe, IPC(Inter Processes Communication), Queue, and Eventcount. The design of C-POREL will follow the characters of UNOS.

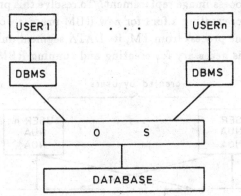

Fig. 2. The structure of one process per user.

2.2. The process structure of C-POREL

According to the architecture of C-POREL. In order to avoid the compiler module working in the multitasks, the compiler module (NOA & NUA) should run in separate process for each user to translate RDBL into RML. The compiler module processes are created by separate users.

In each node TM is the DDBMS Scheduling Management Program of the transactions, the TM must be kept constantly in the memory. Meanwhile, the TM should create dynamically RBM child processes in accordance with the messages sent by the Compiler Module of local node or the Communication System (CS).

Each RBM process handles only one subtransaction, so TM may manage many RBM processes in each node while DDBMS is in multiuser environment. Fig. 3 shows the Process Structure of C-POREL.

Here the following problems must be resolved:

(1) For the UNIX process management mechanism, the parent and the child processes shared the TEXT segments, but do not share DATA

segments. The DATA segments of the child processes are the copies of the parent. We do not hope that each RBM process which is the child of TM includes the DATA segment of the TM, otherwise the system would have too much redundant memory space. The usual way is to invoke the system call *exec( )* primitive in child process to overlay the process that is running with a new program to avoid this redundancy. But this way is rather expensive, because we have to swap-in the code from the secondary storage and accomplish complex process image replacement. To resolve this problem, the organization of creating a fork for new RBM process would be to split a stand-alone process from TM, its DATA segment only includes the space that is necessary for creating and running RBM.

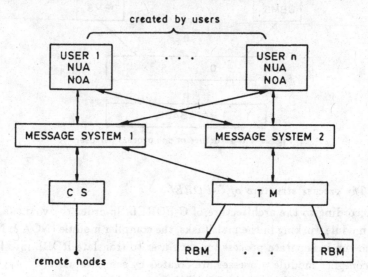

Fig. 3. The process structure of C-POREL at one node

(2) The system catalogs reflecting the system state are the foundation of all analyses, it may be accessed by almost all system modules. In pioneer system POREL, the catalog accesses from all modules are completely carried out by the communication system CS. This uniform structure seems very neat. But this access operation needs interprocess message exchange, common interprocess communication causes the system to pay very expensive cost. To reduce this cost, the short catalog access in compile phase (NUA & NOA) should be carried out separately and organized into a compile process (UNN,

see below). However, the remote nodes catalog access (long catalog requested from NOA) would be performed through the CS module in TM. Here the system has to manage the catalog's concurrency control program to guarantee the consistency. The Optimal Process Structure of C-POREL is shown in Fig. 4 'which is illustrated as follows:

(a) UNN (USER-NUA-NOA) created by the users includes Editing RDBL subroutine. Identification and Authentication, Compilation (NUA & NOA), Catalogs (short & long) query subroutines and Integrity checking. Its message environment is:

 • For message system 1:

 Input: the long catalog messages coming from remote nodes;

 Output: the requests for querying long catalog in the remote nodes;

 • For message system 2:

 Input: the result data or other diagnosis messages of transactions returning to the users;

 Output: the Relational Machine Language (RML) codes and the control messages which are compiled from the RDBL transaction.

(b) RBMO is a process of TM that holds the copy of RBM(k) process image. RBMO is a part of the system kernel of C-POREL. Its functions include creating dynamical RBM(k) child process to respond to the signal sent by TM, and building up the pipe for interprocess communication between RBM(k) and TM. The RBMO is also inside the memory. The RBM(k) process executes one and only one subtransaction and is managed by TM to achieve synchronization among the relative RBM processes in the network wide based on the Two-Phase-Commit (TPC) protocol of DDBMS.

2.3. The concurrency control of C-POREL

In each node, TM manages and coordinates resource request. Here, we describe the concurrency control strategy in accordance with the types of resources.

(A) Short catalog

(1) The process UNN has to query the short catalog at local node. Since the opportunities of changing short catalog are rather small, we will compare the version number of the catalog and use the locking tech-

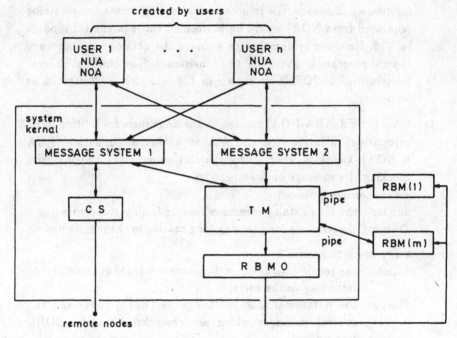

Fig. 4. The optimal process structure of C-POREL at one node.

nique to reduce the interprocess communication. UNN only has to read the short catalog version number at local node before querying the short catalog. After compiling, i.e. the messages of RML codes and the catalog version number that UNN reads have been sent to the TM, TM will compare the version number sent by UNN with current version number of short catalog. If they are not equal or the short catalog at local node has been locked, TM will let the corresponding UNN re-compile the RDBL, otherwise TM will set the short catalog with *Shared Lock* (S-lock) and do not release it until the transaction is committed or backed out.

(2) If the transaction will change the short catalog, UNN has to request the *Exclusive Lock* (X-lock) of short catalog on network wide through the CS. To avoid deadlock, the request must be in accordance with the node's order. We give every node a number to identify it. TM is permitted to request the X-lock of ith node if all of the jth node $(j = 1, 2 \ldots i - 1)$ has been locked. These locks cannot be released until the transaction ends.

(B) Long catalog

(1) For the purpose of optimizing, the UNN in NOA phase may query the long catalog which may stay in a remote node, and only statistics information in long catalog are queried, e.g. the size of subrelation, the number of different attribute value, etc. This query does not set any lock. However, with this strategy, the information of long catalog read by the transaction in UNN phase may differ from the RBM execution phase. Here we base on such a hypothesis: during one subtransaction running from the compile phase (UNN) to the execution phase (RBM), possibility of inserting or deleting many tuples by some other transactions on the same subrelation is small, i.e., the possibility that the statistics information in long catalog will be varied sharply is small. The small changing of statistics information does not affect the system efficiency. Meanwhile, no matter what case will occur, the consistency of DB will not be destroyed by any transaction. In this way, the system saves the overhead of handling some scarce case.

(2) In RBM phase, it may occur that many RBM(k) processes want to change the same long catalog at the same time. These concurrent accesses are not permitted. So some items of long catalog must be set as the critical sections, e.g. access path (B-tree), the addresses of storage segments or pages, etc. C-POREL handles it by setting EVENTCOUNTs which basically simulates semaphore.

(C) Subrelation

C-POREL uses the preclaiming locking strategy and the locking granularity which is subrelation[1]. The locking mode is *Shared Lock*(S-Lock) and *Exclusive Lock*(X-Lock). To avoid the deadlock, the request must follow the node's order: only all ith nodes where $i < j$ have been locked, can the locking of jth node be granted. In this way, the system saves the great expense of checking the deadlock. For the application environment that transactions are not very crowded, this locking strategy can still be reasonable. In the future, we will distinguish the difference of application environment and using other concurrency control strategies such as to include the deadlock checking mechanism or to use the optimistic method.

2.4. Message systems

As most of the operating system, UNOS messages are rather expensive. The cost of message communication is an important factor of affecting system efficiency. In C-POREL, a transaction needs interprocess communication many times, so we must exactly choose the communication tools to dispose message systems.

In UNOS, IPC is a tool of message communication while the amount of messages is rather small, every message volume cannot exceed 100 bytes. For IPC the media is the memory, so its speed is much faster than others. But for the communication with large amount of messages, this tool is not suitable.

Pipe is the communication tool using file buffering which can only be used in internal process communication. Its efficiency depends on the status of file buffering. In general, for communication with large amount of messages, it is more efficient than IPC. To advance communication efficiency, the pipe reading and writing must hold 8*512 bytes as one message unit, so each process which uses the pipe writing needs the private message buffer. It is suitable for interprocess communication between TM and RBM(k).

Queue normally works through the disk file. Because of the slow speed of the secondary storage device, it is not a reasonable tool in the efficiency. But its volume of messages is large, so it is suitable for communication with large amount of messages and which also needs the buffering function. It fits both the MESSAGE SYSTEM 1 and the MESSAGE SYSTEM 2.

2.5. Signal mechanism

UNOS's signal mechanism is an effective tool of process synchronizing management. In Two-Phase-Commit protocol of DDBMS, when the co-ordinator TM receives the nonsuccess message from a subtransaction, all of the relative subtransactions have to backout. Here, TM must use the soft interrupt (invoking *kill*( ) primitive) to force all of the relative RBM processes which execute subtransaction to rollback. The RBM must be preset to the signal interrupt fashion (invoking *signal*( ) primitive). Thus when RBM receives some signals, it will switch immediately to the backout subroutine.

2.6. Process priority

UNIX and UNOS are in accordance with the priority and the state of processes to decide which process images remain in the memory and which process occupies CPU. In C-POREL, the processes are scheduled by OS in light of process scheduling algorithm, as well as by TM. This two scheduling mechanisms must be coordinative to avoid the process that TM allows it to be active while OS suspends it. We can use the OS primitive *setpriority( )* to change process priority to make some concession among the processes possessing equal weight. When TM communicates with a RBM(k) process, TM must set the RBM(k) process's priority higher than others. It will keep this priority until the end of the communication. And when some processes want to access critical sections, TM must increase the process priority so that it can access the critical section.

At the beginning when the system has been started, the priority of C-POREL processes will be set in the order of TM, CS, RBMO, RBM(k), UNN. Thus the priviledged TM can handle each state promptly. Otherwise, TM can set each priority of RBM(k) higher or lower in accordance with greater or lesser urgency request of each transaction.

2.7. Consistency control

DDBMS must ensure that any Database access of the transactions is consistent. On the multi-subtransaction state, the consistency control is based on the Two-Phase-Commit protocol. Otherwise, TM must be able to ensure node robustness. In C-POREL, local node recovery is accomplished by TM in accordance with the security point of database at local node and TA, STA tables which record the system environment. The network recovery is carried out through the cooperation of TM in all nodes, it includes resending messages to failure node and receiving ACK. Since UNOS does not provide enough recovery functions, the Log and relative tables recording the system environment must remain in the stable storage.

2.8. Conclusion

The flexibility and powerful functions of UNIX and its compatible versions provide necessary environment to design DDBMS. But as most of the current operating systems, the service agents of UNIX and UNOS cannot completely satisfy the special requirements of DDBMS, e.g. they have no shared data segments and no I/O block management needed by DDBMS. The message overhead appears rather expensive, and no special scheduling classes for DDBMS are provided which are necessary to solve the problm of process queueing mentioned in Ref. 4. It is our hope that UNIX and its compatible versions will be prefered to DDBMS when they are more powerful.

References

1. Zhou Longxiang, "The distributed relational database management system C-POREL", *Scientia Sinica, Series A*. Vol. XXIX, No. 1 (Jan. 1986) 78-91.
2. Th. Härder, *The Implementierung von datenbanksystemen*, Hanser Verlag, 1978.
3. B. Walter & E. Neuhold, *POREL: A Distributed Database System*, IEEE-CS Press, 1984.
4. M. Stonebreaker, "Operating system support for database management", *Communication of ACM* **24**, No. 7.
5. Zhou Longxiang, "The strategy of catalog management of distributed relational database management system C-POREL", *Proc. of pre VLDB* (Aug. 1986).
6. Zhou Longxiang, "The transaction management of distributed relational database management system C-POREL", *Scientia Sinica* **6** (Jun. 1988) 665-672.
7. S.R. Bourne (Bell Lab.), *The UNIX System*, Addision-Wesley Publishing Company.
8. CRDS, *UNOS Internal Manual*, 1984.
9. J.W. Schmidt & M.L. Brodie, *Relation Database System Analysis and Comparison*, Springer-VBHN, 1983.
10. *The RDBL Text*, Technical Report of Inst. of Math., Acad. Sinica. and Shanghai Univ. of Science & Technology.

IUC: AN INTERFACE FOR UNDERSTANDING CHINESE LANGUAGE*

Li Xiaobin
Institute of Software, Academia Sinica

Abstract

This paper describes a general interface for understanding Chinese technical materials — IUC. It is of good adaptability and can be used in many application domains. Enriched by some background knowledge, it can understand Chinese technical materials and extract important information according to the user's requirements. Currently, it is applied to understand Chinese glaucoma medical records. The information obtained by it is used by a machine learning program to construct an expert system.

Natural language is any language that human learn from their environment and use to communicate with each other. It shows the special intelligence of humans. Chinese has a long history and is one of the most widely used natural languages in the world. Chinese is different from Western languages in pronunciation, written form, vocabulary and grammar.

In Chinese, the logical relationship between character and character, or word and word, or sentence and sentence, depends on their order, their

---

*Supported by the TWAS Research Grant.

meaning and some function words. The syntactic and semantic features of words play the main role in determining the logical relationships among words in a sentence. Chinese is a root-isolated and analytic language without inflection. Chinese words have no inflection, no matter in what positions they appear in the sentence. A written Chinese sentence is a line of consecutive Chinese characters which contains no marks helping to segment words and phrases. All these peculiarities have made Chinese very difficult for computer processing, but on the other hand, it is these difficulties that have made the understanding of Chinese very attractive.

IUC is a general interface for understanding Chinese technical materials and can be used in many application domains. Enriched by some essential knowledge related to the application domain and some information requirements, IUC is capable of accepting Chinese technical materials from Chinese character terminals and extracting the required information on the basis of understanding these materials. IUC is implemented with 6000 lines of PASCAL code and run on the microcomputer UNIVERSE 68. We have applied it to understand Chinese glaucoma medical records and have achieved good results (see Appendix II).

1.1. The Overall Structure of IUC

The major modules of IUC are monitor and those modules which perform the functions of word segmentation, syntactic and semantic analysis, meaning understanding and knowledge base maintaining. A knowledge base is included in IUC. The overall structure of IUC is showed in Figure 1.

Some background knowledge related to the Chinese language and the application domain must be put into the knowledge base by the maintenance module before IUC goes in operation. Under the control of monitor, each Chinese technical material is read sentence by sentence, and then every sentence in the text is segmented into a sequence of words by the 'segmentation module', this sequence of words is later transformed into a meaning structure of the sentence by the analysis module. Finally, the understanding module decides the referents for pronouns and abbreviations in order to make the meaning structure perfect and extracts the required information from the whole set of perfect meaning structures of this Chinese text.

The knowledge in the knowledge base is necessary for all the above phases. Due to the characteristics of Chinese, technical Chinese in particular, IUC processes a Chinese text at different levels, accordingly, the knowledge base is also divided into several parts (see Figure 2):

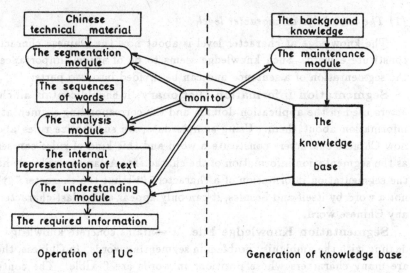

Operation of IUC   Generation of knowledge base

Legend :

☐☐☐☐ : Permanent files
⬭⬭⬭⬭ : Temporary files
◯◯◯◯ : Program module
⟶ : Flow of data
⟹ : Flow of control   Fig. 1

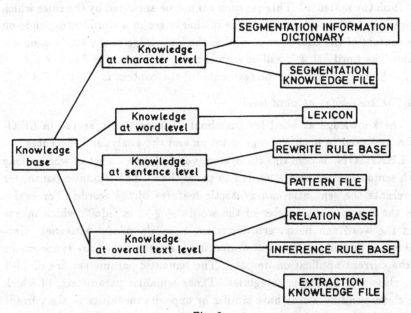

Fig. 2

(1) The knowledge at character level

The knowledge at character level is about how the Chinese characters constitute a word. Such knowledge seems to be of special importance in the segmentation of a sentence and can be divided into two parts:

Segmentation Information Dictionary. It should contain all characters used in the application domain and the corresponding segmentation information about them. Using sample data, we summarize rules about how Chinese characters constitute a word and this kind of rules can serve as the segmentation information of the characters. As an example, we have the segmentation information of a character "们" that the character "们" is not a word by itself and besides, it can only appear as the last character in any Chinese word.

Segmentation Knowledge File. It contains concrete knowledge for dealing with the ambiguity problem in segmenting words. In Chinese, there are many characters whose positions in words are flexible. The context within a Chinese sentence and the knowledge involved in the application domain must be considered when we segment the sentence into a sequence of words. For example, the Chinese character "常" appears in many words, e.g. "非常", "常规", etc. If the sentence looks like "…非常规范…", how do we know which one of the two words "非常" and "常规" should be segmented out from the sentence? This question cannot be answered by the rules which concern only the possible positions of characters in a word. It depends on the context of the character as well as the knowledge of the application domain. The word "非常" will be segmented if the context is "非常规范化" while the word "常规" will be segmented if the context is "非常规范围内".

(2) The knowledge at word level

The knowledge at word level is about Chinese words, stored in LEXICON and used in both the segmentation and the analysis of sentences.

LEXICON. It contains the system vocabulary — a set of words along with semantic parameters needed to parse them. The semantic parameter represents the semantic and syntactic features of the words. For example, the semantic parameter of the word "感觉", is "ida0" which means that the word can be a verb describing people's mental activities. Several words may share the same semantic parameter if they are synonymous in the current application domain. The semantic parameters are divided into classes — semantic categories. Those semantic parameters, of which the corresponding words have similar or opposite meanings in the current application domain, belong to the same semantic category.

(3) The knowledge at sentence level

The knowledge at this level includes grammar and the knowledge concerning the deep structure of sentences. Grammar of a language is a scheme for specifying the sentences allowed in the language, including the rules for combining words into phrases and clauses. The deep structure of a sentence is an internal representation which describes the meaning of the sentence.

This kind of knowledge is used in the analysis of sentences and divided into two parts:

Rewrite Rule Base. It contains semantic grammar rules, or as is called here, rewrite rules. They describe phrases and clauses in terms of the semantic categories in the domain being discussed. The nonterminal symbols are the names of sets of semantic parameters and the terminal symbols are the semantic parameters. By applying sequences of rewrite rules, a sequence of semantic parameters that corresponds to the word sequence of a sentence can be derived from the start symbol. For example, in the current domain, we have defined rewrite rules like this:

⟨medical record sentence⟩ ::= ⟨history sentence⟩ |

⟨examination sentence⟩

⟨history sentence⟩ ::= ⟨time⟩⟨person⟩⟨symptom clause⟩ | ...

⟨symptom clause⟩ ::= ⟨location⟩⟨symptom⟩ | ...

Pattern File. The knowledge related to the deep structure of sentences is stored in this file. The deep structure used by IUC is case frame. For the semantic parameter of each word in LEXICON, there is a case frame in this file provided the word can be used as a predicate. In the deep structure of a sentence in which a word is used as a predicate, there are only a few cases allowed to occur. All such cases, and the semantic restrictions on how to fill slots of these cases, are contained in the case frame corresponding to this word.

(4) The knowledge at overall text level

This is the knowledge related to the domain being discussed. Technical Chinese allows ellipsis of which the meaning can be figured out only if additional knowledge about the domain being discussed is provided. In addition, the required information is often implied in Chinese technical materials. Without the help of such knowledge, it is sometimes impossible to decide the referents for pronouns and abbreviations and extract the required information. This kind of knowledge is applied in the phase of information extraction and divided into three parts:

Relation Base. It contains the knowledge about the relations between two semantic parameters and between two case frames in the application domain. For example, let x and y be two semantic parameters and x contain y, we can define a relation "contain" to describe the relation between x and y, put contain (x, y) into Relation Base.

Inference Rule Base. It contains a set of inference rules which are composed of conditions and results. Both the conditions and the results can be relations or case frames of certain kind. For example, ill(y), contain $(x, y) \implies$ ill(x) is an inference rule which says that the whole organ is considered ill when its part is ill.

Extraction Knowledge File. IUC is to be used to extract information from technical Chinese texts. For each piece of information to be extracted, this file contains its elementary extraction patterns and additional concrete knowledge. For example of extraction knowledge see Appendix I.

1.2. The Segmentation of Sentences

All the written sentences in Chinese are composed of individual characters without any mark to indicate how characters constitute words. There are many possibilities for a single Chinese character to be combined into a word. So it is not easy to segment a Chinese sentence into a sequence of words.

The segmentation of sentences is an operation at character level, by which a reasonable sequence of words is recognized from the sequence of characters in a sentence. It is quite evident that a sentence cannot be segmented only by the help of a lexicon. If a lexicon is consulted to excess in a segmentation phase, the segmentation will be inefficient and the mistakes are hard to avoid, so some information about how the Chinese characters constitute a word is useful in this phase. In addition, observing how people segment Chinese sentences, we find: usually, people can segment sentences that they understand, and often make mistakes if they do not understand them. This fact shows that the segmentation of sentences is closely related to the understanding of sentences and the knowledge about both the context and the domain is very important. The effectiveness of this segmentation is decided by knowledge and the methods of using the knowledge.

Here three kinds of knowledge are introduced in IUC to help the segmentation: SEGMENTATION INFORMATION DICTIONARY, SEGMENTATION KNOWLEDGE FILE and LEXICON which have been discussed above in detail.

The segmentation of sentences is performed by the segmentation module in the following way: Any sentence, as a sequence of characters, is scanned from left to right. When the scan starts, we take the whole sequence of characters as the current sequence and the head of this sequence as the current character. The segmentation information of the current character is selected from SEGMENTATION INFORMATION DICTIONARY and used to figure out a reasonable word of which the current character is the first one. If the segmentation information is not enough, then the segmentation information of the character following the current one will be used. If this is still not enough, then LEXICON will be used to see if the current character starts with a word (or more) which,as a sequence of characters, is identical with a sequence consisting of the first few characters of the current sequence. Knowledge about the context and the application domain will be used if ambiguity occurs (i.e. more than one word is selected). Some complex ambiguity problems can be solved by the user in an interactive way too. Note that the current character is sometimes a word by itself. Once a reasonable word is fixed, the current sequence will be modified by deleting the word from it. If the current sequence is empty, the segmentation of the sentence is completed successfully. Otherwise the head of the current sequence will be the current character and the above steps will be repeated. The segmentation of the sentence in IUC is efficient, because those three kinds of knowledge mentioned above are used. Restricted to the application domain, the segmentation information is very useful so that LEXICON is not often searched for word.

1.3. The Analysis of Sentences

To analyse a sentence, syntax and other sources of knowledge are used to determine the functions of the words in the input sentence in order to create a data structure by which the meaning of the sentence can be obtained and some information needed by the system can be found.

The analysis will start, at word and sentence levels, after the segmentation is completed.

1.3.1. The deep structure of sentence

In 1968, Fillmone proposed the "case frame" consisting of a verb and one or more noun phrases. This knowledge structure should serve as the deep structure of a sentence. A case frame describes the meaning of a sentence better than a derivation tree created according to the formal grammar. But, the same meaning can often be expressed differently with different verbs, thus different case frames may be employed. This weakness of case frame is avoided in IUC by taking into consideration the meaning of the sentences. Thus, the deep structure in IUC is an improved version of Fillmore's case frame to meet the needs of our system. This improved model is called meaning frame model and is defined as follows:

$$\langle \text{text frame} \rangle ::= \langle \text{order} \rangle \langle \text{sentence frame} \rangle \,|$$
$$\langle \text{order} \rangle \langle \text{sentence frame} \rangle \langle \text{text frame} \rangle$$
$$\langle \text{sentence frame} \rangle ::= [\langle \text{relation} \rangle] \langle \text{simple sentence frame} \rangle \,|$$
$$[\langle \text{relation} \rangle] \langle \text{simple sentence frame} \rangle$$
$$\langle \text{sentence frame} \rangle$$
$$\langle \text{order} \rangle ::= \text{positive integer}$$
$$\langle \text{relation} \rangle ::= \langle \text{time relation} \rangle | \langle \text{cause relation} \rangle \,|$$
$$\langle \text{result relation} \rangle | \dots$$
$$\langle \text{simple sentence frame} \rangle ::= \langle \text{predicate} \rangle \langle \text{case} \rangle \langle \text{case element} \rangle \,|$$
$$\langle \text{simple sentence frame} \rangle \langle \text{case} \rangle \langle \text{case element} \rangle$$
$$\langle \text{predicate} \rangle ::= \langle \text{semantic parameter} \rangle | \langle \text{semantic category} \rangle$$
$$\langle \text{case} \rangle ::= \langle \text{agent} \rangle | \langle \text{object} \rangle | \langle \text{time} \rangle | \langle \text{location} \rangle | \langle \text{degree} \rangle | \dots$$
$$\langle \text{case element} \rangle ::= \langle \text{semantic parameter} \rangle | \langle \text{phrase frame} \rangle \,|$$
$$\langle \text{simple sentence frame} \rangle$$
$$\langle \text{phrase frame} \rangle ::= \langle \text{semantic category} \rangle \langle \text{semantic parameter} \rangle \,|$$
$$\langle \text{semantic category} \rangle \langle \text{semantic parameter} \rangle$$
$$\langle \text{phrase frame} \rangle$$

This kind of meaning frame model is special in three aspects:

(1) The deep case slots in a frame are not filled directly with words of the corresponding sentence. Instead, they are filled with semantic parameters of these words. We know, the sentences which express same meaning may be very different not only in their structure but also in their words. These semantic parameters can be viewed as the deep representations of the words and with them, we can free the deep structure from the election of words (the same deep structure can be employed if the same meaning is expressed with different words). These semantic parameters in meaning frame facilitates the connection of the words whose meanings have certain

relations in the current domain and the connection of meaning frames which describe the same meaning.

(2) Since predicates in Chinese are not only verbs, but also adjectives and nouns, we have set up different sorts of case frames for verbs, adjectives and nouns respectively. Our case frame contain some general case slots, such as agent, object, time, location and instrument, and some special case slots needed by the current application system, such as quality, degree and so on.

(3) Besides the case frame associated with a predicate (i.e. simple sentence frame), other frames are introduced, such as phrase frame, sentence frame, text frame and so on, they describe the relations among components of a phrase, a sentence, a text and need not be associated with any predicate.

It needs the support of syntax and other sources of knowledge to map the surface structure of a sentence onto the deep structure of the sentence. What syntax is appropriate for this meaning frame model?

1.3.2. Semantic grammar

While proposing the representation of case frames, Fillmore put forward a case grammar. With a case grammar to analyze a sentence, the determination of case elements mainly depends on the prepositions within the sentence and semantic knowledge about the words in the sentence. But case grammar is not suitable for Chinese. So some Chinese processing systems, in which the internal representation of sentences is case frames, have to make use of the transformational grammars of Chomsky to get a tree structure of the sentence, then to transform this tree structure into case frames. The tree structure of a sentence describes only the syntactic relationships among components within the sentence and it is very difficult to map such a tree structure to the deep structure for expressing the meaning of the sentence.

In IUC, the semantic grammar is adopted to overcome these mapping difficulties. It is possible to organize LEXICON such that words are classified according to semantic as well as syntactic criteria. By writing down a grammar that is specific to a particular domain, one can make the syntactic components to imply more semantic information and facilitate semantic analyses. With the help of system organization strategies, this reduces the problem of ambiguity, makes the overall process more efficient, and makes an effective matching strategy possible for handling ellipsis.

The semantic grammar SG in IUC is defined as follows:

$SG=(Vt, Vn, S, R)$

1) Vt is a finite set of semantic parameters, i.e. a finite set of terminal symbols.

2) Vn is a finite set of semantic categories, i.e. a finite set of nonterminal symbols.

$Vt \cap Vn = \phi.$ $V = Vt \cup Vn.$

3) S is a start symbol. $S \in Vn.$

4) R is a set of semantic grammar rules.

$R = \{uxv \longrightarrow uyv | x \in Vn, u, v \in V^*, y \in V^+$ and $y = \alpha\{P|\varepsilon\}\beta,$
$\alpha, \beta, \in V^*, P \in V$ and P is a predicate$\}.$

The language defined by SG is a set of semantic parameter strings, anyone of these strings is composed of finite semantic parameters. Since every semantic parameter can be associated with a Chinese word, in fact, SG has defined a set of Chinese sentences.

The quality of parsing will be affected by the determination of categories in the semantic grammar. We have proposed the following rules of classfying words:

(1) according to the semantic features of words,

(2) considering the needs of application domain,

(3) avoiding the ambiguity of classification.

The semantic grammar applied by IUC in the domain of glaucoma has grammatical classes like ⟨person⟩, ⟨time⟩, ⟨feel⟩, ⟨symptom⟩, ⟨disease⟩, and so on. Its rewrite rules describe phrases and clauses in terms of these semantics categories.

1.3.3. The analysis and the strategy

The analysis module deals with segmented sentences one by one to set up deep structures of these sentences. It does parsing and semantic analysis in separate stages.

Parsing

All words with their semantic parameters in LEXICON and the semantic grammar rules in REWRITE RULE BASE are needed for parsing to get the tree structure of a sentence which describes the syntax structure of the sentence and implies more semantic information. Top-down processing and depth-first search is chosen for parsing.

Two issues about parsing:

Efficiency. Parsing proceeds in recursive manner and does backtracking frequently. Some useful heuristic information must be added to guide the backtracking and make the parsing more efficient. Because parsing is a top-down process and its ultimate aim is to match a derivation tree with a semantic parameter string of the sentence to be parsed (the given string for short), we might as well use this given string to reduce the set of possible SG rules during parsing in the following way: Before parsing, we build a derivation set for each nonterminal symbol (i.e. semantic category), this derivation set contains all semantic parameters which the corresponding nonterminal symbol can derive. When a SG rule is elected during parsing of the sentence, for every terminal symbol (i.e. semantic parameter) in the rule, the parser looks for its counterpart in the given string, and for every nonterminal symbol in the rule, the parser checks whether any member of its derivation set has its counterpart in the given string. If there is any symbol in the rule which cannot find a counterpart in the given string, the rule is shown to be useless, otherwise the rule should be tried in the parsing of the sentence. In this way, some useless rules are picked out before they are employed and the backtracking is guided by the derivation sets, so the efficiency of the parsing is improved.

Ambiguity. The problems of ambiguity have been reduced by using SG rule. Apart from the artificial ambiguities which are due to inappropriate classification of semantic categories, others are almost all due to polysemy. A polysemant has many meanings and is associated with many semantic parameters in IUC. We can define different priorities for the semantic parameters of the polysemant according to their frequencies of application in the domain. With these priorities, we can give priority to the consideration of the common meaning in the domain. Once a semantic parameter of the polysemant is taken into consideration, we must check up on whether it is congenial with other components of the given string and consider another semantic parameter of the polysemant if it is not suitable in the sentence. In this way, the problem of ambiguity about polysemy can be solved.

For example, the Chinese sentence "昨日患者發現右眼疼痛" is parsed in the following way:

First, the semantic parameters of all words in the sentence will be found from LEXICON after the sentence is segmented:

昨日	患者	發現	右	眼	疼痛
Ca23	Aa00	Gb02	Cb03	Bk03	Ia00

Then with SG, a derivation tree of the sentence can be gotten by parsing:

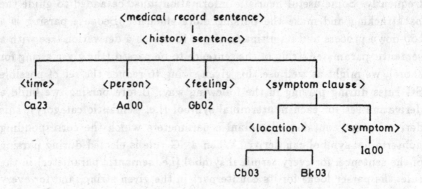

Note: A predicate is marked with "*".

Semantic analysis

The semantic analysis is also a recursive process for choosing appropriate components from the tree structure of a sentence built by the parser and fitting them into the case slots of the case frame that describes the meaning of this sentence.

The semantic analysis of a sentence begins at the top level of the tree structure of the sentence and then goes down to other levels of this tree in turn. In every level of the tree structure, the terminal symbols will be examined to see whether they are predicates. If there is a terminal symbol serving as a predicate at this level, the case frame associated with it will be fetched from PATTERN FILE and the case slots of this case frame will be filled with suitable components at this level or its ancestral levels, according to the information contained in this case frame to show what case slots can occur in the frame and the semantic restrictions for filling these case slots. Otherwise, a phrase frame will be constructed and every component at this level will be fitted into the slots of this phrase frame. If there are nonterminal symbols filled into the slots after the frame (the case frame or the phrase frame) has been built up at this level, the similar analysis will go on respectively at the descendent levels of the nonterminal symbols and the frames returned will replace the nonterminal symbols. The semantic analysis will continue in this way until the case frame of the sentence is set up, in which the case slots are only filled with terminal symbols, (i.e. semantic parameters) or other frames.

For example, a deep structure of the above Chinese sentence can be built up by semantic analyses:

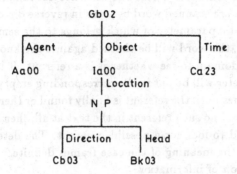

Note: A phrase frame is marked with "NP", it is filled with the semantic parameters of all components in the phrase and their corresponding semantic categories.

1.4. Understanding Chinese Text

We have shown in the above how the analysis of sentences is done. In fact, there are some problems in the two stages of analysis. There may be certain pronouns and abbreviations in the text for which the corresponding slots of the frames have no actual values at all (the semantic parameter of pronoun is not considered as an actual value) so that these frames cannot express the meaning of the sentence clearly. In addition, much information needed by user is often implied in a set of case frames of the text and cannot be discovered directly. The cause of these problems is the lack of context and background knowledge. The understanding module is designed for solving these problems. The knowledge at text level is applied in this process and is composed of three parts, namely RELATION BASE, INFERENCE RULE BASE and EXTRACTION KNOWLEDGE FILE which have already been mentioned in 1.1.

The understanding module accomplishes the following tasks:

(1) The determination of the referents

The understanding module determines the referent for each pronoun or abbreviation in a sentence, fetches an appropriate component from the context of this sentence and assigns it to the corresponding empty slot of the case frame of the sentence. Every case frame will be checked for empty slots after all case frames of the Chinese text have been built up. The semantic restrictions of the empty slots are used to determine the semantic category of the referents. To find the referents of a particular pronoun or abbreviation, all sentences before the sentence containing the pronoun or the abbreviation are scanned word by word in reverse direction. If there is a word, the semantic parameter of which belongs to the semantic category of the due referent, the word will be checked against the knowledge related to the application domain to see whether it is a referent. It it is a referent, its semantic parameter will be put in the corresponding empty slot. Otherwise, scanning continues until the referent is finally found or there is nothing to be scanned. If there is no such referent in the text at all, then domain inference rules will be used to look for a possible referent. The determination of the referents makes the meaning of the case frames definite.

(2) The extraction of information

The information will be extracted by the understanding module from the case frames of the Chinese text to satisfy the needs of the application system. This extraction makes use of the knowledge at text level and the strategy of combining backward reasoning with search.

To extract a piece of information, a set of elementary patterns about this piece of information in EXTRACTION KNOWLEDGE FILE, some semantic parameters related to certain cases of the elementary pattern in RELATION BASE and some inference rules in INFERENCE RULE BASE will be used to derive a lot of new patterns from which this piece of information can arise. With this set of new patterns and the elementary patterns, we all examine one by one a series of case frames produced from the text to find some case frames which can match one pattern in this set. Finally, this piece of information will be extracted from these case frames and be returned to the system according to its needs.

1.5. Conclusion

IUC is an interface for understanding Chinese technical materials. It is knowledge-based and uses multiple knowledge sources, especially domain-specific knowledge. IUC has the following salient features:

(1) IUC demonstrates an increased flexibility while retaining precision in parsing elliptical sentences and those sentences that are not quite grammatical.

(2) The complexity of semantic analysis can be reduced by IUC. The semantic analysis can be controlled at a suitable degree to satisfy the needs of application domain exactly and raise efficiency.

(3) The problem of ambiguity in languages cannot be evaded completely, nevertheless, IUC can reduce and solve some problems of ambiguity in

technical Chinese processing by applying a variety of knowledge related to the domain or interacting with the user.

(4) The redundant information can be removed during the extraction phase of an IUC.

(5) IUC can examine the input sentences one by one, find their mistakes promptly and refer these mistakes to user.

Of course, on the other hand, Chinese sentences understood by IUC are limited in the current domain due to the application of the domain-specific knowledge. But this kind of limitation is not in contradiction with good adaptability of IUC. All kinds of knowledge in IUC are separated from the program modules and located in the knowledge base along. IUC can be applied in anyone of the domains by changing its knowledge base.

Currently, IUC has been applied in a glaucoma diagnosis domain to understand Chinese medical records and extract some information according to the requirement of user.

Acknowledgement

The author is very grateful to his tutor Prof. Lu Ruqian for his good suggestions and valuable help during the writing of this paper.

References

1. Avron Barr and Edward Feigubaum, *The Handbook of Artificial Intelligence*, Vol. 1, 1981.
2. N.J. Nilssion, *Principles of Artificial Intelligence*, 1980.
3. T. Winograd, *Language as a Cognitive Process*, Vol. 1, 1983.
4. Mary Dee Harris, *Introduction to Natural Language Processing*, 1985.
5. B. Bruce, "Case system for natural language", *Artificial Intelligence* **6** (1975).
6. 管紀文、谷新英,《結合上下文輔助分詞的學習系統》, 1982。
7. 朱德熙,《語法講義》, 1981。
8. 吳竟存、侯學超,《現代漢語句法分析》, 1982。
9. 梅家駒等,《同義詞詞林》, 1983。

Appendix I
User requirements in glaucoma domain

(1) Personal state (sex):
   1. M   2. F

(2) Disease History (non_glaucoma):
   1. no   2. iritis   3. cataract   4. hormone_taking
   5. corneal_trauma

(3) Disease History (glaucoma):
   1. no   2. primary_glaucoma   3. secondary_glaucoma
   4. cogenital_glaucoma

(4) Symptom (head_ache):
   1. no   2. moderate   3. severe

(5) Regular Exam (vision):
   1. 1.5   2. 1.2   3. 1.0   4. 0.9   5. 0.8   6. 0.7   7. 0.6   8. 0.5   9. 0.4
   10. 0.3   11. 0.2   12. 0.1   13. 0.01   14. light_perception   15. blind

(6) Conjuntiva (congest):
   1. no   2. slight   3. moderate   4. severe

(7) Conjuntiva (scar):
   1. (−)   2. (+)   3. (++)   4. (+ + +)

(8) Conjuntiva (nipple):
   1. (−)   2. (+)   3. (++)   4. (+ + +)

(9) Conjuntive (bubble):
   1. (−)   2. (+)   3. (++)   4. (+ + +)

(10) corneal (foggy_oedema):
   1. no   2. slight   3. moderate   4. severe

(11) corneal (opacity):
   1. no   2. slight   3. moderate   4. severe

(12) corneal (diameter):
   1. small   2. normal   3. big

(13) corneal (vessel_):
   1. (−)   2. (+)   3. (++)   4. (+ + +)

(14) corneal (KP):

1. (−)   2. (+)   3. (++)   4. (+ + +)

(15) Anterior Chamber (depth):
1. deep   2. slight_shellow   3. shellow   4. vanish

(16) Anterior Chamber (centre_ACD):
1. >4CT   2. 3.5CT   3. 3CT   4. 2.5CT   5. 2CT   6. <1.5CT

(17) Anterior Chamber (peripheral _ ACD):
1. >1CT   2. 1/3CT   3. 1/4CT   4. <1/4CT

(18) Pupil (diameter):
1. small   2. normal   3. big

(19) Pupil (circular):
1. yes   2. no

(20) Pupil (light_reaction):
1. sensitive   2. slow   3. fixed

(21) Pupil (block_adhesion):
1. no   2. yes

. . . . . .
. . . . . .

The information requirements of user are composed of 74 items like that.

Appendix II

Two instances in glaucoma domain

(1) Two Chinese medical records

病歷1：

劉　　　　男　　76歲　　C－174774

79－9－13

　　近三個月來雙眼視力下降。

　　查：雙眼不充血，雙角膜尚清。前房正常。雙瞳孔等圓，對光反應存在。雙晶體前皮質可見水泡。眼底：右乳頭大小正常，色較正，其周可見脈胳膜弧。黃斑區呈灰黃，盤狀，略隆起2D左右，其上有新生血管爬行，其周暗紅出血。網膜V充盈，A顯細，且有交叉壓迫症。眼底豹紋狀。左乳頭色較灰白，血管偏向鼻側，乳頭周有脈胳膜弧。網膜V充盈，A變細，交叉症可見。黃斑區較暗，中心凹光反射不顯。眼底豹紋狀。

● 視力　右眼：0.1

　　　　左眼：0.1

● 眼壓　右眼：20.55

　　　　左眼：20.55

● 視野檢查：

視野：右3/1000中心暗點。左5/1000中心及5/330周邊與生理盲點相連環形暗點，有鼻側階梯。

● 眼壓二十四小時曲線：右眼差值：　7.45

　　　　　　　　　　　　左眼差值：11.25

● 眼壓描記：右眼　C：0.07

　　　　　　　　　　F：1.05

　　　　　　　　　　P O/C：

　　　　　　　左眼　C：0.13

　　　　　　　　　　F：1.82

　　　　　　　　　　P O/C：

● 前房角鏡：右眼：W，W，W，W

　　　　　　左眼：W，W，W，W

兩眼呈大寬角。

● 診斷：雙開角型青光眼。

病歷2：

郭　　　　女　　65歲　　C－302839

85－10－15

　　患者三天前左眼突然疼痛，頭痛，視力下降。診為急性青光眼。眼壓不能控制，而且惡心、嘔吐。

　　查：右球結膜不充血。角膜透明，橫徑9.5mm，KP（－）。前房淺，閃光（－）。瞳孔直徑3.5mm，鼻下方瞳孔緣後粘連，晶體核棕黃色，混濁。眼底：視乳頭色澤正常，邊界清楚，C/D等於0。視網膜血管大致正常。黃斑中心反光彌散。左眼結膜中度混合充血。角膜輕度霧狀水腫，橫徑9.5mm。前房淺，閃光（＋）。瞳孔中度大。晶體核棕黃色，混濁。眼底窺不入。

● 視力　右眼：0.4
　　　　左眼：光感
● 眼壓　右眼：7.5
　　　　左眼：31
● 前房角鏡：右眼：N3,N4,N2,N2
　　　　　　左眼：N4,N4,N4,N4
● 診斷：右原發性閉角型青光眼慢性期。左原發性閉角型青光眼急性發作期。

(2) Two information lists extracted by IUC from the two Chinese medical records:

About first record:

Right eye:

(1) Personal State (sex):　1. M
(5) Regular Exam (vision):　12. 0.1
(30) Yellow Pot (reflection):　2. weak
(31) Retina Vascular (A_pulsate):　2. yes
(32) Retina Vascular (AV_cross):　2. yes
(33) Retina (bloody):　2. yes
(34) Retina (pigment_pot):　2. less
(37) Visual Field (loss):　3. degree 2
(39) Symptom (visual_failing):　2. slowly
(41) OSC (a_width):　1. W
(42) OSC (b_width):　1. W
(43) OSC (t_width):　1. W
(44) OSC (n_width):　1. W
(50) Disease History (diagnosis):　6. angle open glaucoma
(61) Personal State (age):　76
(62) Regular Exam (IOP):　21
(70) IOP_depict (C):　0.07
(71) IOP_depict (F):　1.1
(73) IOP_curve (scope):　8

Left eye:

(1) Personal State (sex):　1. M
(5) Regular Exam (vision):　12. 0.1
(29) Optic Cop (color):　2. light
(30) Yellow Pot (reflection):　2. weak
(31) Retina Vascular (A_pulsate):　2. yes
(32) Retina Vascular (AV_cross):　2. yes

(34) Retina (pigment_pot): 2. less

(37) Visual Field (loss): 5. degree 4

(39) Symptom (visual_failing): 2. slowly

(41) OSC (a_width): 1. W

(42) OSC (b_width): 1. W

(43) OSC (t_width): 1. W

(44) OSC (n_width): 1. W

(50) Disease History (diagnosis): 6. angle open glaucoma

(61) Personal State (age): 76

(62) Regular Exam (IOP): 21

(70) IOP_depict (C): 0.14

(71) IOP_depict (F): 1.9

(73) IOP_curve (scope): 12

About second record:

Right eye:

(1) Personal State (sex): 1. F

(5) Regular Exam (vision): 9. 0.4

(15) Anterior Chamber (depth): 3. shellow

(21) Pupil (block-adhesion): 2. yes

(30) Yellow Pot (reflection): 2. weak

(40) Symptom (sick): 2. yes

(41) OSC (a_width): 4. N3

(42) OSC (b_width): 5. N4

(43) OSC (t_width): 3. N2

(44) OSC (n_width): 3. N2

(50) Disease History (diagnosis): 7. angle close glaucoma

(52) Lens (opacity): 2. opaque

(61) Personal State (age): 65

(62) Regular Exam (IOP): 8

(63) Optic Cup (C/D): 0

Left eye:

(1) Personal State (sex): 1. F

(3) Disease History (glaucoma): 2. primary_glaucoma

(4) Symptom (head_ache): 2. moderate

(5) Regular Exam (vision): 14. light_perception

(6) Conjuntiva (congest): 3. moderate

(10) Corneal (foggy_oedema): 2. slight

(15) Anterior Chamber (depth):   3. shellow
(18) Pupil (diameter):   3. big
(38) Symptom (eye_ache):   3. moderate
(39) Symptom (visual_failing):   3. abruptly
(40) Symptom (sick):   2. yes
(41) OSC (a_width):   5. N4
(42) OSC (b_width):   5. N4
(43) OSC (t_width):   5. N4
(44) OSC (n_width):   5. N4
(50) Disease History (diagnosis):   7. angle close glaucoma
(52) Lens (opacity)L   2. opaque
(61) Personal State (age):   65
(62) Regular Exam (IOP):   31

KJ-8920 Vector Recognition System (KJVR)

Cheng Hu

Institute of Software

Academia Sinica

Li Gang

Institute of Computing Technology

Academia Sinica

Abstract

KJ-8920 Vector recognition system is one system software of the large computer KJ-8920. This system can recognize the parallel components in the DO loop body in Fortran program automatically, and rewrite the parallel components into the vector form which can be executed in parallel on KJ-8920.

This system is completed on VAX/785, in C language. It can be transported to the peripheral computer of KJ-8920. As it acts as an independent system, separated from vector Fortran compiler, it can be modified and strengthened easily.

The system has high efficiency and strong function, making best use of KJ-8920 parallel hardware features.

In order to rewrite the DO loop, we expand the definition of identifier and label defined in Fortran-77. The identifier or label formed by adding symbol "♯" before the standard identifier or label is permitted, which can be recognized by Vector-Fortran compiler too.

The paper aims to present system's structure and its general function.

115

1. The Parallel Hardware Features of KJ-8920 Large Computer

1.1. *Before we introduce the KJVR, it is necessary to know some parallel hardware features of the KJ-8920*

KJ-8920 has 16 vector registers. Each register has 64 components. Each component has 64 bits. These registers are used to store vectors, provide operands for the vector operation device. Each register has also component-point register V_p, which always points to the present component. When vector instruction is executed, V_p's content is 0, then getting each component from register will lead to the increase of V_p's content.

The computer has vector-length register VL, which has 8 bits, used to count the length of the vectors and control the dynamic combination of vector registers.

When VL's content is equal or less than 64, there are 16 vector registers which can be numbered V0, V1,... ,V16. Every register has 64 bits at this time.

When the VL's content is larger than 64, there are only 8 vector registers which are numbered V0, V1... ,V7. At this time, V0,... ,V7 is formed by connecting V0, V8; V1, V9;... ;V7, V15. Every register has 128 bits.

1.2. *The type of vector processing*

In KJ-8920, there are three types of vector processing which are horizontal, vertical, and horizontal-vertical. But the main vector processing type is horizontal-vertical.

Because of the dynamic combination of vector registers, if the length of vector is less than 128, vector can be processed vertically.

1.3. *Segment of vector*

Since every register has 64 bits, the computer permits two registers to connect. If the length of vector is over 128, the vector must be segmented, each segment must be less or equal to 128. Suppose the length of vector is N, the vector can be segmented as following:

$$N = 128r + q \quad r \geq 0, \quad q < 128$$

q can be regarded as one segment if the registers needed by computer is over 8. The vector, the length being N, can be segmented like this:

$$N = 64r1 + q1 \quad r1 \geq 0, \quad q1 < 64$$

$q1$ can be regarded as one segment.

Here we do not want to talk about other parallel hardware features such as pipeline and reduction of vector processing device.

2. KJ-8920 Vector Recognition Systems's Structure

KJVR is an independent system separated from vector-Fortran compiler. It can be modified and strengthened easily. The system is mainly composed of seven parts as follows:

a. Pre-processing module

b. Overall-control module

c. Program-process module

d. The judgement of basic condition module

e. Implicit data dependency recognition module

f. Apparent data dependency recognition module

g. Rewriting loop body module

The system structure is as follows:

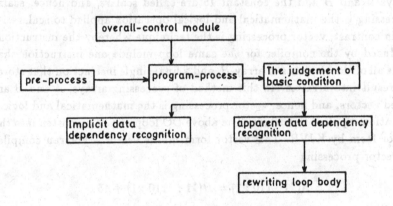

(KJVR's structure diagram)

3. Vectorization

Vector processing is the computer's ability to perform operations on arrays of data simultaneously. In contrast, the scalar processing used by most computers deals with only one operation and one element at a time. In order to raise the computer's speed, the more vector processing operation, the better.

Program loops occur frequently within scientific and technical application programs. A simple DO loop in the Fortran is shown below that adds 15 to each element of array B and stores the sum in array A. The loop

control variable I is used as the index into arrays A and B, and ranges
from 1 to 110 in increments of 1, using contiguous memory locations:

$$\text{DO } 10 \; I = 1, 110$$
$$10 \; A(I) = B(I) + 15$$

In traditional scalar computer systems, the machine instruction produced by the compiler for this example is a sequential issue of instruction
that loads individual elements of array B, then adds 15, and stores the
result into array A. The loop control variable I is increased by 1, and each
step in the loop is then tested for completion. If any part of the loop is
in completion for any given instruction, the compiler "branches" back into
the loop to compile the omission.

Each of the five steps of this loop – load, add, store, increment, test
and branch – are repeated over and over on each element of array B until
I equals 110. In this method of processing arrays, the single elements of
arrays A and B and the constant 15 are called scalars, and hence, scalar
processing is the mathematical and logical operation applied to scalars.

In contrast, vector processing is the technique whereby the instructions
produced by the compiler for the same loop include one instruction that
loads all of the elements of array B, and a final single instruction that stores
the result into array A. In this method of processing arrays, A and B are
called vectors, and hence, vector processing is the mathematical and logical
operations applied to vectors. The above DO loop can be rewritten into the
vector form by KJVR. This vector form makes vector – Fortran compiler
do vector processing

$$A(^*1:110:1) = B(^*1: \;\; 110:1) + 15$$

Vector has the following form in KJVR

$$P(^*e1:e2:e3)$$

P is the identifier, $e1, e2, e3$ are integer expressions.

4. Data Dependency

KJVR aims to recognize the parallel components in DO loop body and
rewrite loop body into vector form. The vector form can be executed simultaneously. But in Fortran program, there are many loops which cannot
be rewritten into the vector form. The following is a simple example:

$$A(1) = 1$$
$$A(2) = 2$$

$$A(101) = 101$$
$$\text{DO } 10 \; I = 1, 100$$
$$A(I + 1) = A(I)$$
10   CONTINUE

If the DO loop is executed sequentially, the result is:

$$A(1) = A(2) = \ldots A(101) = 1$$

If we rewrite the loop body into the vector form $A(*2 : 101 : 1) = A(*1 : 100 : 1)$, then execute it simultaneously. The result of execution will be:

$$A(1) = 1$$
$$A(2) = 1$$
$$A(3) = 2$$

$$A(101) = 100$$

The later result is different from the former result. Obviously, the later result is wrong. In the array A, as the loop control variable I increases, the value of element $A(I + 1)$ is dependent on that of $A(I)$, and then renewed. This process of renewing $A(I + 1)$ must be a sequential process. If we write the loop body into vector form, the dependency of $A(I + 1)$ on $A(I)$ will be eliminated. Because the vector form statement is executed simultaneously. The dependency of elements of array is called data dependency. Before we rewrite the loop body into the vector form, the data dependency in the loop must be taken account of.

5. Examples to Evaluate the KJVR's General Functions

5.1. Recognition of data dependency caused by EQUIVALENCE, COMMON statement

In Fortran program, COMMON and EQUIVALENCE statement may cause data dependency in loop body. This kind of data dependency, sometimes called implicit data dependency, has two features:

(a) The data dependency was caused by statement outside the loop.

(b) The domain of COMMON and EQUIVALENCE statements is beyond the DO loop.

As we know, vector recognition is a transformational system which changes the program from one form to another form. But the correctness must be guaranteed in the domain.

```
SUBROUTINE KJ1
DIMENSION A(100), B(200)
EQUIVALENCE(A, B)
```

C-Original–Code–

```
        DO 3 I = 1, 100
        A(I) = 1
        B(2*I) = 2
3       CONTINUE
        END
```

C-Vectorized–Code–

```
        B(*2 : 200 : 2) = 2
        A(*1 : 100 : 1) = 1
        I = 101
3       CONTINUE
        END
```

The above example demonstrates the data dependency caused by EQUIVALENCE statement. KJVR has changed the order of the statement $A(I) = 1$ with statement $B(2*I) = 2$ to eliminate the data dependency and write the loop body into vector form automatically.

```
SUBROUTINE KJ2
DIMENSION A(100), B(100)
DIMENSION C(200), D(100)
EQUIVALENCE (A, C)
EQUIVALENCE (A, D)
COMMON//A, B
```

C-Original–Code–

```
        DO 10 I = 1, 100
10      B(I) = C(I + 99)
        DO 11 J = 1, 99
```

```
        D(J) = B(J)
11      CONTINUE
        END
```

C-Vectorized-Code-

```
        DO 10 I = 1, 100
10      B(I) = C(I + 99)
        D(*1 : 99 : 1) = B(*1 : 99 : 1)
        J = 100
11      CONTINUE
        END
```

The relation of array A, B, C, D, is shown in the following figure

A(100)	B(100)

C(200)

D(100)

The element of array on the same horizontal line has the same physics storage.

In the loop DO 10, the assignment statement $B(I) = C(I + 99)$ equals the $C(I + 100) = C(I + 99)$. The later exists data dependency, so DO 10 cannot be vectorized. The assignment statement $D(J) = B(J)$ in DO 11 has no data dependency. It can be vectorized.

```
        SUBROUTINE KJ3
        DIMENSION A(100, 100)
        EQUIVALENCE (I, M)
```

C-Original-Code-

```
        M = 1
        DO 10 I = 1, 100
        A(M, I) = 3.1416
10      CONTINUE
        END
```

C-Vectorized-Code-

```
        M = 1
        A(*1 : 100 : 1, *1:100:1) = 3.1416
```

```
        I = 101
10      CONTINUE
        END
```

In DO10, you cannot vectorize the $A(M, I) = 3.1416$ into $A(M,^* 1 : 10 : 1) = 3.1416$.

5.2. Recognition of data dependency caused by statement functions

Statement functions occur frequently in FORTRAN program. Sometimes it can cause data dependency

```
        SUBROUTINE KJ4
        REAL A(100), B(100), C(100)
        SF1(K) = A(K) + B(K) + C(K)
```

C-Original–Code–

```
        DO 1 I = 1, 99
        A(I + 1) = SF1(I)
1       CONTINUE
        DO 2 J = 1, 100
        B(J) = SF1(J)
2       CONTINUE
        DO 3 M = 2, 100
        C(M − 1) = SF1(M)
3       CONTINUE
        END
```

C-Vectorized–Code–

```
        DO 1 I = 1, 99
        A(I + 1) = SF1(I)
1       CONTINUE
        B(*1 : 100 : 1) = A(*1 : 100 : 1) + B(*1 : 100 : 1)
        1 + C(*1 : 100 : 1)
        J = 101
2       CONTINUE
        C(*1 : 99 : 1) = A(*2 : 100 : 1) + B(*2 : 100 : 1)
        1 + C(*2 : 100 : 1)
        M = 100
3       CONTINUE
        END
```

In loop 1, the loop body is $A(I + 1) = SF1(I)$ which is equivalent to $A(I+1) = A(I)+B(I)+C(I)$. The statement $A(I+1) = A(I)+B(I)+C(I)$ caused data dependency. So it cannot be vectorized.

5.3. Loop distribution

In loop body, some statements cause data dependency or prevent other statements from being vectorized. At this time, we can divide one DO loop into several DO loops, then try to vectorize these loops. This technique is useful in KJVR.

```
SUBROUTINE KJ5
REAL A(100), B(100), C(100)
```

C-Original-Code-

```
      DO 10 I = 1, 100
      A(I) = B(I) + C(I)
      B(I) = B(I)/C(I) + 1
      WRITE (9, 100) B(I)
10    CONTINUE
      END
```

C-Vectorized-Code-

```
      A(*1 : 100 : 1) = B(*1 : 100 : 1) + C(*1 : 100 : 1)
      B(*1 : 100 : 1) = B(*1 : 100 : 1)/C(*1 : 100 : 1) + 1
      DO # 101 I = 1, 100
      WRITE (9, 100) B(I)
#101  CONTINUE
```

The WRITE statement prevents the whole loop from being vectorized. So separate the WRITE statement from loop 10.

```
SUBROUTINE KJ6
DIMENSION A(101), B(101), C(101)
```

C-Original-Code-

```
      DO 10 I = 1, 100
      A(I) = B(I)*C(I)
      B(I) = A(I)*C(I)
      C(I) = A(I - 1)*B(I - 1)
10    CONTINUE
      END
```

C-Vectorized–Code–

$$A(*1:100:1) = B(*1:100:1)^*C(*1:100:1)$$
$$B(*1:100:1) = A(*1:100:1)^*C(*1:100:1)$$

DO #101 $I = 1,100$

$$C(I) = A(I-1)^*B(I-1)$$

#101 CONTINUE

END

The data dependency is caused by the assignment statement $C(I) = A(I-1)^*B(I-1)$. The whole DO 10 loop cannot be vectorized. So separate the $C(I) = A(I-1)^*B(I-1)$ from DO 10.

5.4. Loop interchange

Generally, KJVR vectorizes the innermost loop in nested loops. In many cases, there exists data dependency in the innermost loop or if we exchange the innermost loop with the next innermost loop, we can improve the performance of vectorized form execution. In this cases, we may exchange the innermost loop with next innermost loop.

SUBROUTINE KJ7

DIMENSION $AA(100,100), B(100,100)$

DIMENSION $CC(100,100), D(100)$

C-Original–Code–

DO 10 $I = 1, M$

DO 10 $J = 1, N$

$$AA(I, J+1) = B(J) + CC(I, J-1)$$
$$CC(I, J) = AA(I, J)^*D(I)$$

10   CONTINUE

END

C-Vectorized–Code–

DO 10 $J = 1, N$

$$AA(*1:M:1, J+1) = B(J) + CC(*1:M:1, J-1)$$
$$CC(*1:M:1, J) = AA(*1:M:1, J)^*D(*1:M:1)$$
$$I = M + 1$$

10   CONTINUE

END

There exists data dependency in the innermost loop, so exchange the innermost loop with the next innermost loop.

```
SUBROUTINE KJ8
DIMENSION A(100), B(100, 100), C(100, 100)
DIMENSION CC(100, 100), DD(100, 100), EE(100, 100)
```

C-Original-Code-

```
      DO 10 I = 2, 300, 2
      DO 10 J = 2, 11, 2
      BB(I, J) = CC(I, J) + DD(I, J)
      EE(I, J) = DD(I - 1, J - 1)
      FF(I, J) = (BB(I, J) + EE(I, J))/2
10    CONTINUE
      DO 11 I = 1, N
      DO 11 J = 1, M
      A(I) = A(I) + B(I, J)*C(I, J)
11    CONTINUE
      END
```

C-Vectorized-Code-

```
      DO 10 J = 2, 11, 2
      BB(*2 : 300 : 2, J) = CC(*2 : 300 : 2, J)
      1 + DD(*2 : 300 : 2, J)
      EE(*2 : 300 : 2, J) = DD(*1 : 299 : 2, J - 1)
      FF(*2 : 300 : 2, J) = (BB(*2 : 300 : 2, J) + EE(*2 : 300 : 2, J))/2
      I = 302
10    CONTINUE
      DO 11 J = 1, M
      A(*1 : N : 1) = A(*1 : N : 1) + B(*1 : N : 1, J)*C(*1 : N : 1, J)
      I = N + 1
11    CONTINUE
      END
```

In nested DO 10, if do not exchange the innermost loop with the next innermost loop, vectorize the loop body. The loop body will be executed by 150 times. Now the loop body is executed by 10 times.

In nested DO 11, exchanging the innermost loop with next innermost loop will improve the performance.

5.5. *Scalar assignment statement expanding*

KJVR can expand the variable in the left side of assignment statement in DO loop.

```
SUBROUTINE KJ9
DIMENSION A(100), B(100), C(100)
```

C-Original–Code–

```
      DO 10 I = 1, 100
      X = A(I) − B(I)
      Y = A(I) + B(I)
      C(I) = X*Y
10    CONTINUE
      END
```

C-Vectorized–Code–

```
      REAL # LV001(100), # LV002(100)
      # LV001(*1:100:1) = A(*1 : 100 : 1) − B(*1 : 100 : 1)
      # LV002(*1:100:1) = A(*1 : 100 : 1) + B(*1 : 100 : 1)
      C(*1 : 100 : 1) = #LV001(*1 : 100 : 1)*#LV002(*1 : 100 : 1)
      X = #LV001(100)
      Y = #LV002(100)
      I = 101
10    CONTINUE
      END
```

5.6. *The original value of loop control variable*

The KJVR vectorize the Fortran program statically. The original value of loop control variable cannot be caculated sometimes, for the following DO loop

```
      DO 2 I = N, M
      loop body
2     CONTINUE
```

The value of N has much impact on the judgement of data dependency. Generally, the value of M has nothing to do with the judgement of data dependency in loop body except some special occasion. KJVR has used the dynamic method to deal with the judgement of data dependency when the value of N is not constant

```
      SUBROUTINE KJ10
      REAL A(100), B(100)
      EQUIVALENCE (A, B)
```

C-Original-Code-

```
      DO 10 I = N, M
      A(I) = 1
      B(2*I) = 2
10    CONTINUE
      END
```

C-Vectorized-Code-

```
      IF(N.LE.0)
      A(*N : M : 1) = 1
      B(*2*N : 2*M : 2) = 2
      ENDIF
      IF (N.GT.0)
      B(*2*N : 2*M : 2) = 2
      A(*N : M : 1) = 1
      ENDIF
      I = M + 1
10    CONTINUE
      END
```

5.7. Control variable

There are many DO loops which have more than one control variable in loop body. KJVR can vectorize this kind of loop.

```
      SUBROUTINE KJ11
      DIMENSION A(K1), B(K1), C(K1), X1(K2), X2(K2)
```

C-Original-Code-

```
      DO 10 I = L, U
      A(I + I1) = X1(I2)
      I2 = I2 + 2
      B(I5*I) = X2(I7)
      I7 = I7 + 3
10    CONTINUE
```

```
      END
```

C-Vectorized–Code–

$$A(*L + I1 : U + I1 : 1) = X1(*I2 : (U - L)*2 + I2 : 2)$$
$$B(*L + I5 : U*I5 : I5) = X2(*I7 : (U - L)*3 + I7 : 3)$$
$$I2 = I2 + (U - L)*2$$
$$I7 = I7 + (U - L)*3$$

```
10    CONTINUE
      END
```

5.8. IF statement

KJVR can vectorize the loop which has IF arithmetic statements and three-branch arithmetic IF statements in loop body, because vector-Fortran compiler has provided the KJVR with the vector form statement of this kind of statement

```
      SUBROUTINE KJ12
      DIMENSION A1(1000), B1(1000), C1(1000)
```

C-Original–Code–

```
      DO 10 I = 1, 1000
      A1(I) = 1.0
      C1(I) = 0.0
10    CONTINUE
      DO 11 I = 1, 1000
      IF(I.LE.200) THEN
      C1(I) = A1(I)*2000.0+ COS(A1(I))
      B1(I) = B1(I)*C1(I)**4/A1(I)
      ENDIF
      IF ((I.GT.200).AND.(I.LE.400)) THEN
      C1(I) = A1(I)+ COS(A1(I))
      B1(I) = B1(I) + C1(I)
      ENDIF
      IF (I.GT.4000) THEN
      C1(I) = A1(I) + 2000.0
      B1(I) = B1(I)**4
      ENDIF
11    CONTINUE
```

```
        END
C-Vectorized-Code-
        A1(*1 : 1000 : 1) = 1.0
        C1(*1 : 1000 : 1) = 0.0
        I = 1001
10      CONTINUE
        WHERE(# LLVC(*1:1000:1).LE.200)
        C1(*1:1000:1)=A1(*1 : 1000 : 1)*2000.0+ COS(A1(*1:1000:1))
        B1(*1:1000:1)=B1(*1 : 1000 : 1)*C1(*1 : 1000 : 1) **4/A1(*1 : 1000 : 1)'
        ENDWHERE
        WHERE((# LLVC(*1:1000:1).GT.200).AND.
      1 (# LLVC(*1:1000:1).LE.400))
        C1(*1:1000:1)= A1(*1 : 1000 : 1)+ COS(A1(*1:1000:1))
        B1(*1:1000:1)= B1(*1 : 1000 : 1) + C1(*1 : 1000 : 1)
        ENDWHERE
        WHERE(# LLVC(*1:1000:1).GT.400)
        C1(*1 : 1000 : 1) = A1(*1 : 1000 : 1) + 2000.0
        B1(*1 : 1000 : 1) = B1(*1 : 1000 : 1)**4
        ENDWHERE
        I = 1001
11      CONTINUE
        END
```

The above example illustrates KJVR's ability to process IF statement.
LLVC is a temporary array added by KJVR automatically.

6. Conclusion

KJVR has been used in coal and oil ministry. It has been proved that KJVR has a strong function and high efficiency. But there are much to be desired to improve the performance and meet the practical needs.

Acknowledgement

We thank Yia Ke-rong, Chen Wang-xiang, Lan Zhi-dong and other people who have worked for the KJVR.

References

1. GB-3057-1982 (ISO 1539-1980, ANSI×3.9-1978), *Programming Language FORTRAN*.
2. Zhang Zhaoqing, Cheng Hu, Chen Shuqing, Liu Kuanming, "Vector Fortran language and its compiler system design", *Chinese Journal of Computer* **4:3** (1981).
3. Fan Zhihua, *et al.*, "Implicit data dependence in vectorization", *Chinese Journal of Computer* **8:5** (1985).
4. L. Lamport, "The parallel execution of DO loops", *Comm. of the ACM* **17:2** (1974).
5. L. Lamport, "The coordinate method for the parallel execution of DO loops", 1973 Sagamore Computer Conference on Parallel Processing.
6. Yukihiko Karaki, "Supercomputer and matrix calculation", 情報處理 **28:11** (1987).

FEL FORMULA – AN ECONOMICAL LAW IN FORMATION OF TERMS

Feng Zhiwei
Fraunhofer-Gesellschaft, IAO
Rosenbergstrasse 28, D-7000 Stuttgart 1
West Germany

Summary

In this paper, author proposed a FEL formula to describe the economical law in formation of terms: the product of economical index E of terminological system and the average length of L of terms exactly equals the formation frequency F of words composing these terms, i.e., $F = EL$. This formula is simple and effective.

In China, a lot of scientists call "term" as "noun". It is not suitable. In reality, most of the terms in natural science and technology are not nouns. Science and technology are developing with each passing day, and new scientific conceptions are emerging in an endless stream. It is impossible to give every new scientific conception a new noun, in overwhelming majority of cases, we combine the individual words to form the word groups (i.e. phrases) in order to express these new conceptions. Therefore the term is not only noun, most of terms must be phrases which are composed of

131

several individual words.

Now a Chinese terminological databank GLOT-C is developing in Fraun-hofer-Institute at Stuttgart. This databank is established on the VAX 11/750 by UNIX operational system and INGRES relational database. In GLOT-C, there are 1510 terms in the field of data processing. We can divide them into two types: word-terms and phrase-terms.

The word-term is the term which includes only single word, e.g. noun, verb, ...etc. In GLOT-C, there are 375 word-terms which include only 244 nouns. The phrase-term is the term which composed of two or more words, e.g. noun phrase, verb phrase, ...etc. In GLOT-C, there are 1135 phrase-terms. The proportion of phrase-term is 75.17%, but the proportion of word-terms is 24.83% and the proportion of noun-terms (a part of word-terms) is only 16.15%. Thus we cannot call the term as noun indiscreetly.

When we look at the terminological system from the viewpoint of lin-guistics, the individual words are the materials of terms (including the word-terms and the phrase-terms), and the terms are the products which are produced by these individual words. In GLOT-C, the sum of word-terms and phrase-terms is 1510, these 1510 terms are produced from 858 different words. All the terms are produced from fewer different words. We will refer to such efficiency as "economical principle of term formation".

In this paper, we will discuss three basic conceptions of "economical principle of term formation": the economical index of system, the formation frequency of words and the average length of terms, and we will propose a FEL formula to express the mathematical relation among them.

1. Economical Index of System

In order to describe these three basic conceptions, first of all, we give several definitions for the following terms which will be used in this paper.

(i) Number of terms: The sum of different terms in terminological sys-tem, i.e. the volume of system. It is represented by T. The unit of T is "item".

(ii) Absolute frequency of word: The occurring times (or used times) of an individual word in the system. It is represented by α. The unit of α is "time".

(iii) Number of different words: The number of different words with a same absolute frequency. It is represented by ν. The unit of ν is "word".

(iv) Sum of different words: The sum of different words with various absolute frequencies in the system. It is represented by W. The unit of W is "word".

$$W = \Sigma \nu$$

(v) Number of running words: The product value of number of different words ν with a same absolute frequency and this absolute frequency α. It is represented by ρ. The unit of ρ is "word-time".

$$\rho = \alpha \nu$$

(vi) Sum of running words: The sum of running words with various absolute frequencies. It is represented by R. The unit of R is "word-time".

$$R = \Sigma \rho = \Sigma \alpha \nu$$

The economical index of a terminological system can be considered as the quotient value obtained when the number of terms T is divided by the sum of different words W. We represent it by E. So we have

$$E = T/W . \tag{1}$$

The unit of E is "item/word" (read as "item per word").

In most of the terminological system, we have $E > 1$; if $E \leq 1$, it means that the system has a lower economical efficiency.

In GLOT-C system, $T = 1510, W = 858,$

$$E = T/W = 1510/858 = 1.76 .$$

When $T = 1510$, the economical index of system GLOT-C is 1.76, every individual word can averagely compose 1.76 items of terms, so this system possesses a higher economical efficiency.

The economical index of terminological system is influenced by the number of terms in the system. The increasing rate of the economical index becomes higher and higher along with the increasing of the number of terms in the system. In GLOT-C, when the number of terms in system is 500 and the sum of different words is 342, its economical index is 1.46; when the number of terms in system is increased to 1000 and the sum of different words increased to 588, its economical index becomes 1.70; when the number of terms in system is increased to 1510 and the sum of different words increased to 858, its economical index becomes 1.76 (see Table 1):

Table 1

T	W	E
500	342	1.46
1000	588	1.70
1510	858	1.76

The number of terms in system gives a strong influence upon the economical index (see Fig. 1).

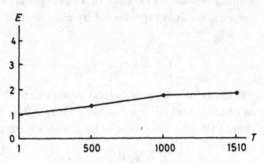

Fig. 1. Influence of *T* on *E*.

In a certain scientific domain, a terminological system with great number of terms would have a great economical index, and in this system, there will be a great number of phrase-terms that are composed of a fewer basic words, and the phrase-terms will become the majority of this terminological system.

2. Formation Frequency of Words

The absolute frequency of every word in terminological system is not the same. There are high-frequency words which occurred very often, and there are low-frequency words which occurred very rarely. Increasing the number of terms, the number of high-frequency words generally also increases, but the occurrence possibility of the new words becomes less and less. Despite the increase of the number of terms, the increasing rate of the sum of different words gradually becomes slower and slower, the high-frequency words will occur repeatedly. There is a function relation between the number of terms T and the sum of different word W:

$$W = \phi(T)$$

This function can be roughly representd in the following diagram (see Fig. 2):

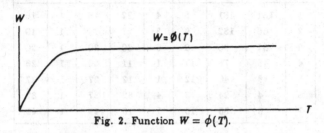

Fig. 2. Function $W = \phi(T)$.

The more high-frequency words the terminological system has, the more terms can be produced by these high-frequency words. The ability of words for producing the terms can be described by formation frequency of words.

The formation frequency of words can be defined as the quotient value obtained when the sum of running words is divided by the sum of different words in a terminological system:

$$F = R/W . \qquad (2)$$

Here F is formation frequency of words. The unit of F is "time". In fact, because the unit of R is "word-time", the unit of W is "word", so the unit of F will be "word-time/word" which is equal to "time".

In (2) the value of F cannot be less than 1, i.e., $F \geq 1$, and, for same terminological system, the value of F cannot be less than the value of E, i.e., $E \leq F$, because there is always $T \leq R$.

In system GLOT-C, the sum of running words that occurs in the 1510 terms is 3216, and the sum of different words that produces 1510 terms is 858, i.e. $R = 3216, W = 858$, thus

$$F = R/W = 3216/858 = 3.75 .$$

When $T = 1510$, the formation frequency of words in system GLOT-C is 3.75. Every individual word can be averagely repeated 3.75 times. Thus this value can also represent the average frequency that these words are used in producing the terms.

The formation frequency of words are also influenced by the number of terms in the terminological system.

In system GLOT-C, when the volume of system includes 500 terms ($T = 500$), the frequency list of words is as below (see Table 2):

Table 2

α	ν	ρ	α	ν	ρ	α	ν	ρ
1	181	181	8	4	32	16	1	16
2	66	132	9	3	27	19	1	19
3	32	96	10	6	60	20	1	20
4	19	76	11	1	11	26	1	26
5	8	40	12	1	12	27	1	27
6	4	24	13	4	52	37	1	37
7	5	35	15	1	15	49	1	49

In this case,

$$W = \Sigma\nu = 342$$

and
$$R = \Sigma\rho = 987$$

thus
$$F = R/W = 987/342 = 2.89 .$$

When the volume of system includes 1000 terms ($T = 1000$), the frequency list of words is as below (see Table 3):

Table 3

α	ν	ρ	α	ν	ρ	α	ν	ρ
1	295	295	12	6	72	25	1	25
2	103	206	13	2	26	26	1	26
3	54	162	14	2	28	29	1	29
4	36	144	15	2	30	33	1	33
5	19	95	17	2	34 .	37	1	37
6	16	96	19	1	19	48	1	48
7	12	84	20	1	20	51	1	51
8	10	80	21	1	21	52	1	52
9	6	54	22	1	22	64	1	64
10	6	60	23	1	23			
11	2	22	24	1	24			

In this case,

$$W = \Sigma\nu = 588$$

and
$$R = \Sigma\rho = 2072$$

thus
$$F = R/W = 2072/588 = 3.52 .$$

When the volume of system includes 1510 terms ($T = 1510$), the frequency list of words is as below (see Table 4):

Table 4

α	ν	ρ	α	ν	ρ	α	ν	ρ
1	411	411	13	5	65	26	2	52
2	150	300	14	3	42	27	2	54
3	73	219	15	2	30	33	2	66
4	52	208	16	3	48	34	1	34
5	44	220	18	1	18	35	1	35
6	24	144	19	3	57	44	1	44
7	14	98	20	1	20	47	1	47
8	14	112	21	2	42	55	1	55
9	13	117	22	1	22	56	1	56
10	5	50	23	2	46	63	1	63
11	8	88	24	3	72	68	1	68
12	7	84	25	2	50	79	1	79

In this case,

$$W = \Sigma\nu = 858$$

and

$$R = \Sigma\rho = 3216$$

thus

$$F = R/W = 3216/858 = 3.75 \ .$$

We can have the following (see Table 5):

Table 5

T	W	R	F
500	342	987	2.89
1000	588	2072	3.52
1510	858	3216	3.75

The increase of the formation frequency of words is along with the increase of the number of terms (see Fig. 3).

In Fig. 3 the dotted line expresses the changing situation of economical index, we can see, for the same number of terms, the value of formation F of words is no less than the value of economical index E, i.e. $F \geq E$. Only when the number of terms $T = 1$, there is only one word in system, F is equal to E, and in other case, F is always greater than E.

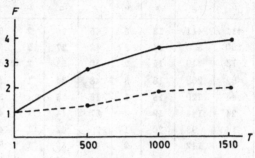

Fig. 3. Influence of T on F.

From Tables 2, 3 and 4, we can see that the increase of absolute frequency of words (i.e. α) always accompanies the decrease of the number of different words with the same absolute frequency (i.e. ν). This relation can be described in the following diagram (see Fig. 4).

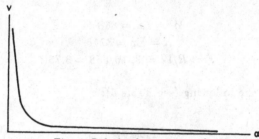

Fig. 4. Relation between α and ν.

It means that the high-frequency words occupy only a little part of the sum of different words in the terminological system, but they can produce a lot of terms. In Table 4, the number of high-frequency words (absolute frequency $\alpha \geq 10$) is 62, the sum of their running words is 1342, the proportion of their running words sum to the sum of all running words in Table 4 is 41.4%. These 62 high-frequency words produced 41.4% running words included in the terms of system GLOT-C. The more high-frequency words are in terminological system, the higher formation frequency of words this system can have.

3. Average Length of Terms

The length of a term is the number of words which are included in this term. In a terminological system, the minimum value of length of term is 1. The length of word-term is always 1, it includes only one word, e.g. the length of term "chengxu" (program) is 1. The length of phrase-term is always more than 1, e.g. the length of term "chengxu sheji" (programming) is 2, the length of term "shuzi zifu ziji" (numeric character subset) is 3, the length of term "tiaojian kongzhi zhuanyi zhiling" (conditional control transfer instruction) is 4, the length of term "pingjun wu guzhang gongzuo shijian" (mean time between failure) is 5, the length of term "si fen zhi yi pingfang chengfaqi" (quarter-squares multiple) is 6, ... etc. From the view point of the economical principle of terminology, if the length of term is too long, it is not practical to use and to remember. Thus it is necessary to study the problem of term length.

In accordance with the economical principle of terminology, in this connection, we propose the conception "average length of term".

In a terminological system, the average length of terms can be described as the quotient value obtained when the sum of running words R is divided by the number of terms T:

$$L = R/T . \tag{3}$$

Here L is the average length of terms. The unit of L is "word-time/item" (read as "word-time per item of terms").

In (3), the value of L is always greater than 1, i.e. $L \geq 1$. In the system where every term is composed of one word, $L = 1$, in other cases, $L > 1$.

In system GLOT-C, $R = 3216, T = 1510$, so we have

$$L = R/T = 3216/1510 = 2.130 .$$

It means that in system GLOT-C, when the number of terms is 1510, every term is composed averagely of 2.130 word-times per item of terms.

The average length of terms seems to have an increasing trend along with the increase of the number of terms. When the number of terms is 500, the average length of terms is 1.974; when the number of terms is 1000, the average length of terms is 2.072; when the number of terms is increased to 1510, the average length of terms also increases to 2.130. Of course, the average length of terms cannot be too long, every terminological system can adjust automatically its average length to an optimum value. In this adjusting procedure, some long terms will be abandoned, some too short terms will possibly be lengthened, and the average length of terms will be relatively steady.

4. Economical Law of Term Formation — FEL Formula

We have discussed three main conceptions in the formation of terms – the economical index E of a system, the formation frequency F of words and the average length L of terms. Now we discuss further the relation among the three conceptions. From the results of experiment in system GLOT-C, we can find out that the product of the economical index E of system and the average length L of terms equals fortunately the formation frequency F of words.

The experimental data as as below (see Table 6):

Table 6

T	E	L	$E \times L$	F
500	1.46	1.974	2.88304	2.89
1000	1.70	2.072	3.52140	3.52
1510	1.76	2.130	3.74880	3.75

From these data of experiment in Table 6, we can establish the following mathematical relation on E, L and F:

$$E \times L = F .$$

When $T = 500$, we have $E \times L = 2.88304$, and $F = 2.89$; when $T = 1000$, we have $E \times L = 3.52140$, and $F = 3.52$; when $T = 1510$, we have $E \times L = 3.74880$, and $F = 3.75$. The value of $E \times L$ equals approximately the value of F.

In fact, due to

$$E = T/W \qquad (1)$$

and

$$F = R/W \qquad (2)$$

(2) ÷ (1), we have

$$F/E = R/T . \qquad (4)$$

According to the definition of average length of terms

$$L = R/T . \qquad (3)$$

Comparing (4) and (3), we can obtain

$$F/E = L$$

thus

$$E \times L = F . \qquad (5)$$

Algebraic expression (5) corresponds with the results of experiment as we mentioned above.

By this reason, we propose the economical law of term formation as follows:

In a terminological system, the product of the economical index E of system and the average length L of terms is exactly equal to the formation frequency F of words composing these terms.

This economical law of term formation can be expressed by a formula:

$$F = EL \tag{6}$$

We call (6) as FEL formula.

From FEL formula, we can draw the following inferences:

(i) In a terminological system, when the average length L of terms is definite, the formation frequency F of words is positively proportional to the economical index E of system. The more is the economical index E of system, the more will be the formation frequency F of words. This relation can be seen clearly from the Fig. 3. In this case, FEL formula becomes

$$F = \kappa_1 E$$

κ_1 is a constant.

(ii) In a terminological system, when the economical index E of the system is definite, the formation frequency F of words is positively proportional to the average length L of terms. The longer the average length L of terms, the higher will be the formation frequency F of words composing these terms. In this case, FEL formula becomes

$$F = \kappa_2 L$$

κ_2 is a constant.

It means that in order to increase the formation frequency of words, we have to lengthen the average length of terms, because the economical index of system is definite, every word can only be included in a definite number of terms.

(iii) In a terminological system, when the formation frequency F of words is definite, the economical index E of system is negatively proportional to the average length L of terms. The increase of economical index E of system will cause the shortening of average length L of terms, and the decrease of economical index E of system will cause the lengthening of the average length L of terms. In this case, FEL formula becomes

$$EL = \kappa_3$$

κ_3 is a constant.

It means that in the condition of not changing the formation frequency of words, if we want to increase the economical index of system in order to make every word to form more terms, then we have to decrease the number of words that are included in some original terms. Because the sum of running words is unchangeable in this case, we must take out a part of words from original terms (generally longer terms) to produce new terms and that will cause the increase of the number of terms. As a result, the number of words included in some terms of the terminological system will possibly decrease and the length of the new term obviously cannot be too long. Consequently the average length of terms in system will be shortened.

Therefore it can clearly be seen that our formula FEL reflects the economical principle and the reasonable relation among the economical index of system, the formation frequency of words and the length of terms in the formation of terms, it is the economical law governing the term formation. Undoubtedly this economical law plays an importat role in the study of formation of terms.

From FEL formula, we can obtain

$$E = F/L .$$

It means that there are two ways to increase the economical index of a terminological system:

(i) Shortening the average length of terms in condition of not changing the formation frequency of terms;

(ii) Raising the formation frequency of words in condition of not changing the average length of terms.

Generally speaking, in a terminological system, it is better to avoid too great a change of the average length of terms. Because the great change of the average length of terms will cause the terminological system to be changed beyond recognition. Due to this reason, the better way to increase the economical index of system is raising the formation frequency of words in condition of basically not changing the average length of terms. By this way, a lot of phrase-term will be produced in the process of formation of terms, the number of phrase-term will become greater than the number of word-terms. In the system GLOT-C, the proportion of phrase-terms is 75.17%, they constitute the majority of term number in the system. This phenomenon is exactly the effect of the economical law of term formation.

ON THE STRUCTURE OF MODELS OF HIERARCHICAL ALGEBRAIC SPECIFICATIONS*

Lin Huimin
Institute of Software
Academia Sinica

Abstract

The structures of some interesting classes of models of hierarchical specifications are analyzed. It is shown that the class of extended models and the class of quotient-initial models of base-complete specification both form complete lattices and there is an isomorphic embedding from the former into the latter.

Key words and phrases: Algebraic specification, abstract data type, consistency, completeness.

1. Introduction

The theory of abstract data types has grown rapidly since the middle of 70's. By now, the algebraic method has been widely accepted as a promising

---

*This work is supported partly by the National Natural Science Foundation of China.

tool in formal specification and development of software systems. It has also been applied to other branches of computer science, such as concurrency and data base theory.

The basic idea of algebraic method is using many-sorted first-order equational theories to specify abstract data types syntactically, so that we can reason about their properties with equational logic. But since the model theory of first-order equational logic cannot be adopted directly to give semantics for data type specifications, several approaches have been proposed to tackle this problem. Among them, the most influential ones are the initial model semantics[1,2,4], final model semantics[10,17] and generated model semantics[3,16]. The initial model approach is most appropriate for the specifications of basic data types (i.e. independent of other types), but it is difficult with this approach to give natural and satisfactory accounts for some phenomena arising from the context of data type extension such as "behavioral equivalence"[5,13,14]. On the other hand, the final and generated model approaches, which are based on the notion of "sufficient completeness", are aimed at hierarchical specifications; but they are not complete in the sense that they have to assume the pre-existence of some basic types such as BOOL which cannot be specified with these methods themselves. Since any real-world specification projects inevitably involve both basic and extended data types, such divergence in semantics created difficulties for practical applications of algebraic specification theory. It is apparent that a uniform treatment of model theory for algebraic specification is urgently needed.

The differences between the initial and final model approaches can be illustrated by the specification of finite sets. Using the initial model semantics, one needs two axioms for the commutative and absorptive laws for the insert operation. But they are not needed if one works with the final model semantics. It is then argued that the latter is preferable since it has more models which are interesting. But little attention has been paid to the difference between two specifications within the framework of final model approach. Both of them are sufficiently complete and their final models are the same, although one of them has two more independent axioms which force its initial model coincide with the final one. These two axioms talk about terms of new sort, but sufficient completeness concerns only terms in the base sorts. In order to distinguish these two specifications and to discuss their relationship, we need a completeness concept which allows us to talk about properties not only in the base sorts but also in the new sort.

It is to this end that we proposed the notion of "relative completeness" in Refs. 11, 12 and several theoretical results were presented there. In this paper, we are going to investigate the structures of models of hierarchical specifications based on this notion. The classes of models we are interested in are extended models and quotient-initial models. The latter is important since, for instance, the well-known "array+pointer" implementation of stack is not a model of the common specification of stack, but is a quotient-initial model of it. We will see that, under certain condition, these two model classes both form complete lattices and the former can be isomorphically embedded into the latter. These results generalize similar work based on sufficient completeness.

The paper is organized as follows. Some basic notations and facts of algebraic specifications are summarized in the next section. Section 3 is a short introduction to the completeness problem in algebraic specification. The structures of some interesting model classes of hierarchical specifications are analyzed in section 4. Section 5 gives examples to illustrate the theoretical results of previous sections. Finally, section 6 summarizes the main contributions of this paper and briefly compares them with other work.

We assume some familarity with universal algebra and category theory.

2. Preliminaries

Most of the notations and concepts used in this paper are more or less standard, so we only give a brief introduction here.

Let S be a set of *sorts*. An S-sorted set is a family $X = \{X^s\}_{s \in S}$ of sets indexed by S. If $S' \subseteq S$ then $X^{S'} = \{X^s\}_{s \in S'}$ is an S'-indexed set. We will often omit superscripts and write $x \in X$ rather than $x \in X^s$ for some $s \in S$.

A *signature* is a pair (S, Σ) where S is the sort set and Σ is a family of sets $\{\Sigma^{w,s}\}_{w \in S, s \in S}$ which gives the function symbols for the signature. We usually simply write Σ for a signature, with the understanding that the sort set for Σ is S, for Σ' is S', etc.

Given a signature (S, Σ) and an S-sorted set of variables X, the S-sorted set of Σ-*terms* over X is denoted by $T_{\Sigma(X)}$. We write T_Σ for $T_{\Sigma(\phi)}$, the set of all *ground* Σ-terms. A *ground instance* of a Σ-term t is a ground term obtained by substituting all variables in t with some ground terms, and similar for ground instances of equations.

A Σ-*equation* is a triple (X, t, t'), where X is a finite set of variables and $t, t' \in T_{\Sigma(X)}$. We usually write $\forall X t = t'$ rather than (X, t, t').

If E is a set of Σ-equations and e a Σ-equation, $E \vdash e$ denotes that e is derivable from E using first-order equational reasoning (see, for example, Ref. 7).

Lemma 2.1.

Let E be a set of Σ-equations and $t, t' \in T_\Sigma$. $E \vdash t = t'$ iff there exist $t_0 \ldots, t_n \in T_\Sigma$ such that $t = t_0, t' = t_n, t_i = v_i[x/u_i], t_{i+1} = v_i[x/u_i']$ where $v_i(x) \in T_{\Sigma(X)}, u_i = u_i'$ or $u_i' = u_i$ is a ground instance of some equation in $E, 0 \leq i < n$.

Let Σ be a signature. A Σ-*algebra* or Σ-*model* $A = (D, \varphi)$ consists of an S-sorted set D and an interpretation map φ which assigns each $f : s_1, \ldots, s_n \to s \in \Sigma$ a function $\varphi(f) : D^{s_1} \times \ldots \times D^{s_n} \to D^s$. We usually write $|A|$ for D and f^A for $\varphi(f)$. We also confuse A and $|A|$, and write, for example, $d \in A$ instead of $d \in |A|$.

A Σ-*homomorphism* h from a Σ-model A to a Σ-Model B is a mapping from $|A|$ to $|B|$ such that for any $f : s_1, \ldots, s_n \to s \in \Sigma$ and $a_1 \in |A|^{s_1}, \ldots, a_n \in |A|^{s_n}$,

$$h^s(f^A(a_1, \ldots, a_n)) = f^B(h^{s_1}(a_1), \ldots, h^{s_n}(a_n))$$

A homomorphism $h : A \to B$ is called an *isomorphism*, denoted $A \cong B$, if there exists a homomorphism $g : B \to A$ such that $g \circ h = id_A$ and $h \circ g = id_B$, where id_A and id_B are identities on A and B, respectively.

It is well-known that there exists a unique Σ-homomorphism from T_Σ (with the standard assignment of functions to function symbols in Σ) to any Σ-model A. We call A a generated-model if this homomorphism is surjective.

Let $\Sigma \subseteq \Sigma'$. A Σ-model A is called a Σ-*submodel* of a Σ'-model A' if $|A| \subseteq |A'|^S$ and for every $f : s_1 \ldots s_n \to s \in \Sigma$, $f^A = f^{A'} \cap |M|^{s_1} \times \ldots \times |M|^{s_n} \times |M|^s$.

A *congruence* relation $\sim$ on a Σ-model A is an equivalence relation on $|A|$ which is compatible with the operations of A, i.e., $a_i \sim b_i \Rightarrow f^A(a_1, \ldots, a_n) \sim f^A(b_1, \ldots, b_n)$ for any $f : s_1 \ldots s_n \to s \in \Sigma$ and $a_i, b_i \in |A|^{s_i}, i = 1, \ldots, n$.

Given a congruence $\sim$ on a Σ-model A, the *quotient* model of A by $\sim$ is denoted by $A/\sim$. Two Σ-models A and B are said to be *quotient-isomorphic* if there exist congruences $\sim_A$ on A and $\sim_B$ on B such that $A/\sim_A \cong B/\sim_B$. Note that if there exists a subjective homomorphism from A to B then A and B are quotient-isomorphic, but not vice-versa.

Let A be a Σ-model. Let also X be an S-sorted set of variables and v a *valuation* map from X to $|A|$. v can be extended uniquely to a map $v^{\natural} : T_{\Sigma(X)} \rightarrow |A|$. For a ground term t, we write t^A for the unique value of t under any valuation.

A Σ-equation $t = t'$ is *satisfied* by a Σ-model A if $v^{\natural}(t) = v^{\natural}(t')$ for any valuation v. A Σ-model satisfies a set of Σ-equations if it satisfies every equation in the set. We write $A \models E$ when A satisfies E and call A a *model* of E.

A (presentation of a) *specification* is a pair $SP = (\Sigma, E)$ where Σ is a signature and E is a set of Σ-equations called the *axioms* of SP. The class of all models of SP forms a category under Σ-homomorphisms, and $T_{\Sigma,E}$, the quotient model of T_{Σ} by the congruence on $|T_{\Sigma}|$ generated by E, is initial in this category.

A *quotient-initial* model of SP is a generated model which has a quotient model isomorphic to the initial model of SP. It is obvious that the initial model is quotient-initial and any two quotient-initial models are quotient-isomorphic. But note that a quotient-initial model of SP need not be a model of SP, i.e., the equations in E need not be satisfied by it.

Lemma 2.2.

Let I_{SP} be an initial model of $SP = (\Sigma, E)$. For any ground Σ-equation $e, I_{SP} \models e$ iff $E \vdash e$.

Notation.

We use Mod_{SP} to denote the class of all models of SP, GM_{SP} for the set of generated models of SP, and QI_{SP} for the set of quotient-initial models of SP.

Definition.

An extended signature is a pair (Σ_b, Σ) of signatures such that $\Sigma_b \subseteq \Sigma$. Call Σ_b the base signature of the extended signature.

An extended specification $SP_e = (SP_b, (\Sigma, E_e))$ consists of a base specification $SP_b = (\Sigma_b, E_b)$ and an extension part (Σ, E_e) such that (Σ_b, Σ) is an extended signature and E_e is a set of Σ-equations.

Notation.

We write $E = E_b \cup E_e$ for the set of axioms of SP_e. For each extended specification SP_e we associate it with a basic specification (Σ, E). When we talk about 'the initial model of SP_e', we mean the initial model of its associated basic specification.

For extended specifications, we are only interested in those models which preserve the initial models of its base specification. This is reflected in the following

Definition.

A model for an extended signature $\Sigma_e = (\Sigma_b, \Sigma)$ is a pair $M_e = (M_b, M)$ such that M is a Σ-model and M_b is a Σ_b submodel of M. Call M_b the base submodel of M. M_e is a generated model for Σ_e if M is a generated model for Σ.

An extended model M of an extended specification $SP_e = (SP_b, (\Sigma, E_e))$ is a generated model (M_b, M) for (Σ_b, Σ) such that M_b is an initial model of SP_b and M satisfies $E = E_b \cup E_e$.

An extended specification is ext-satisfiable if it has an extended model.

Notation.

The set of extended generated models of SP_e is denoted by GM^e_{SP}. We usually write M for an extended model, with the understanding that it has a base submodel M_b.

3. Completeness Problem in Algebraic Specification

At the lowest level of any hierarchical specification there must be some basic specifications. It is natural and widely accepted to adopt the initial model semantics for these basic specifications[1,2,4], which is called the "initiality constraint". This constraint must be respected at higher levels of the hierarchy. The following notion of consistency reflects such requirement:

Definition (Consistency).

An extended specification $SP_e = (SP_b, (\Sigma, E_e))$ is consistent (or E is consistent) iff for any $t, t' \in T_{\Sigma_b}, E \vdash t = t' \Rightarrow E_b \vdash t = t'$.

An arbitrary consistent specification may have many models which behave quite differently. In order for specifications to have manageable behaviours, we ought to impose more requirement on them. "Sufficient completeness" was proposed in Ref. 6 at the early days of abstract data type theory and has been taken as one of the fundamental notions in this field. Most work on hierarchical and parameterised specifications are based on it.

Definition (Sufficient-completeness).

An extended specification $SP_e = (SP_b, (\Sigma, E_e))$ is sufficiently complete iff for any $t \in T^{S_b}$, there exists $t' \in T_{\Sigma_b}$ such that $E \vdash t = t'$.

Note that this definition talks only about base sorts. It does not mention any properties in the new sort. As a consequence, the relationship between initial and final model semantics was obscured, as pointed out in Refs. 11 and 12. A new completeness concept was proposed there:

Definition (Relative-completeness).

An extended specification $SP_e = (SP_b, (\Sigma, E_e))$ is s-relative-complete ($s \in S$ is a sort) iff for any $t, t' \in T_\Sigma^s$, $\{t = t'\} \cup E$ is consistent $\Rightarrow E \vdash t = t'$.

SP_e is a base-complete, or relative-complete, if it is s-relative-complete for every $s \in S_b$, or for every $s \in S$, respectively.

It is proved that sufficient-completeness is strictly stronger than base-completeness. Namely, every sufficiently complete specification is also base-complete, but there are base-complete specifications which are not sufficiently complete.

For more discussions on completeness in algebraic specifications, we refer to Ref. 12. Here we only quote two results from that paper for later use.

Lemma 3.1.

Suppose SP_e is consistent and base-complete.
(1) For any ground equations e and e', if both $\{e\} \cup E$ and $\{e'\} \cup E$ are consistent then $\{e, e'\} \cup E$ is also consistent.
(2) For any $t, t' \in T_\Sigma$, $\{t = t'\} \cup E$ is consistent iff $E \vdash \text{cont}(t) = \text{cont}(t')$ for every base context $\text{cont}(x)$, where a base-context is a one-variable term of a base sort.

Two terms verifying the condition of (2) are called "indistinguishable" since they have the same "visible" computational behavior.

4. Lattice Structure of Hierarchical Models

In this section, we are going to investigate the structures of extended models and quotient-initial models of an extended specification, as well as the relationship between them.

Let Σ be a signature. All Σ-congruence relations on T_Σ forms a complete lattice $(C_\Sigma, \subseteq)$ under set inclusion. For an arbitrary $\sim \in C_\Sigma$, $C_\Sigma \downarrow \sim = \{c \in C_\Sigma : c \subseteq \sim\}$, the set of all *congruences under* $\sim$, forms a complete sublattice of C_Σ. This is also true for $C_\Sigma \uparrow \sim = \{c \in C_\Sigma : \sim \subseteq c\}$, the set of all *congruences over* $\sim$.

A Σ-model M induces a congruence relation $\sim_M$ on T_Σ given by $t \sim_M t'$ iff $M \models t = t'$ for any $t, t' \in |T_\Sigma|$. If M is a generated model, then $M \cong T_\Sigma / \sim_M$.

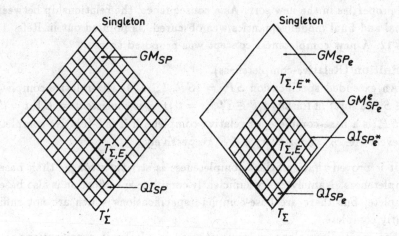

Fig. 1

Let M, M' be Σ-models. We write $M \prec M'$ if there exists a Σ-homomorphism from M to M'. It is well-known that $M \prec M'$ iff $\sim_M \subseteq \sim_{M'}$ for generated models M, M'. So we can 'transfer' the lattice structure of C_Σ to GM_Σ and obtain a complete lattice $(GM_\Sigma / \cong, \prec)$.

Let $SP = (\Sigma, E)$ be a basic specification and M a quotient-initial model of SP. $M \prec T_{\Sigma,E}$ by definition so $\sim_M \subseteq \equiv_E$, i.e. $\sim_M \in C_\Sigma \downarrow \equiv_E$. On the other hand, suppose $\sim \in C_\Sigma \downarrow \equiv_E$, we can define a map $h : T_\Sigma / \sim \longrightarrow T_\Sigma / \equiv_E$ by $h([t]_\sim) = [t]_{\equiv_E}$ for $t \in T_\Sigma$. It is easy to verify that h is well-defined and in fact is a Σ-homomorphism. This shows that $T_\Sigma / \sim$ is a quotient-initial model of SP.

In this way, we obtain a bijection between $(QI_{SP} / \cong, \prec)$ and $(C_\Sigma \downarrow \equiv_E, \subseteq)$. It is easy to see that the bijection preserves ordering. We already know $(C_\Sigma \downarrow \equiv_E, \subseteq)$ is a complete lattice, so this gives

Fact 4.1.

The set of all quotient-initial models of a specification forms a complete lattice under homomorphism (modulo isomorphism), with its initial model being the greatest element (i.e. the initial model is final in the category of quotient-initial models and homomorphisms).

A fact from universal algebra says that $(GM_{SP} / \cong, \prec)$ is isomorphic to $(C_\Sigma \uparrow \equiv_E, \subseteq)$, so the former is also a complete lattice. The situation is pictured in Fig. 1 (left).

In the context of extended specifications, we are more interested in extended models than simple ones, so we extend the above notions accordingly.

In the following discussion we fix a consistent extended specification $SP_e = (SP_b, (\Sigma, E_e))$. We write $\equiv_b$ for the congruence relation on T_{Σ_b} induced by E_b and $\equiv$ for the congruence relation T_Σ induced by $E = E_e \cup E_b$. An extended congruence $\sim$ is a congruence on T_Σ such that $\sim |_{\Sigma_b} = \equiv_b$. Let C_{SP_e} denote the set of all extended congruences on T_Σ.

Fact 4.2.

1. $M \in |GM_{SP_e}^e|$ iff $\sim_M \in C_{SP_e}$.
2. SP_e is consistent iff $\equiv \in C_{SP_e}$.
3. Suppose SP_e is consistent. $(C_{SP_e}, \subseteq)$ is a lower semilattice with the least element $\equiv$, or equivalently, $(GM_{SP_e}^e, \prec)$ is a lower semilattice with the least element T.

Proof.

(1) ($\Rightarrow$) Assume $M \in GM_{SP_e}^e$. M has a base submodel M_b which is an initial model of $SP_b = (\Sigma_b, E_b)$. This means $\sim_{M_b} = \equiv_b$. But $\sim_M |_{\Sigma_b} = \sim_{M_b}$, so $\sim_M |_{\Sigma_b} = \equiv_b$. Hence $\sim_M \in C_{SP_e}$.

($\Leftarrow$) Assume $\sim_M \in C_{SP_e}$. Let M_b be the image of T_{Σ_b, E_b} in M under the unique homomorphism from $T_{\Sigma, E}$ to M. We have $\sim_{M_b} = \sim_M |_{\Sigma_b} = \equiv_b$, showing M_b is an initial model of SP_b. It is trivial to check that M_b is a Σ_b-submodel of M. Hence $M \in GM_{SP_e}^e$.

(2) ($\Rightarrow$) Assume SP_e is consistent. Then

$$\equiv |_{\Sigma_b} = \{t = t' : t, t' \in T_{\Sigma_b}, \ E_e \cup E_b \vdash t = t'\}$$
$$= \{t = t' : t, t' \in T_{\Sigma_b}, \ E_b \vdash t = t'\}$$
$$= \equiv_b$$

This shows $\equiv \in C_{SP_e}$.

($\Leftarrow$) Assume $\equiv \in C_{SP_e}$. For any $t, t' \in T_{\Sigma_b}$,

$$E_e \cup E_b \vdash t = t'$$
$$\Rightarrow (t, t') \in \equiv_{E_e \cup E_b}$$
$$\Rightarrow (t, t') \in \equiv_b$$
$$\Rightarrow E_b \vdash t = t'$$

Hence SP_e is consistent.

(3) From (2) we know $\equiv \in C_{SP_e}$ and it is the least element of C_{SP_e} by definition. So it is suffice to prove that any nonempty subset J of C_{SP_e}

has a greatest lower bound in C_{SP_e}. Let $c = \cap J$ be the intersection of all congruences in J. Then $c|_{\Sigma_b} = \equiv_b$ since for any $j \in J, j|_{\Sigma_b} = \equiv_b$. Hence $c \in C_{SP_e}$, and c is the greatest lower bound of J by its construction.

Theorem 4.3.

Suppose SP_e is consistent and base-complete. $(C_{SP_e}, \subseteq)$ is a complete lattice.

Proof.

Let $SP_e^* = (\Sigma, E^*)$ where $E^* = E \cup \{t = t' : t, t' \in T_\Sigma$ and $\{t = t'\} \cup E$ is consistent$\}$. By Lemma 3.1(1), SP_e^* is consistent. Let $\equiv^*$ be the congruence relation on T_Σ induced by E^*. $\equiv^* \in C_{SP_e}$. Furthermore, for any $\sim \in C_{SP_e}$,

$$t \sim t' \Rightarrow \{t = t'\} \cup E \text{ is consistent}$$
$$\Rightarrow t = t' \in E^*$$
$$\Rightarrow t \equiv^* t'$$

Hence $\sim \subseteq \equiv^*$. In other words, $\equiv^*$ is the maximal element of C_{SP_e}. Combine with fact 4.2(3), this shows that $(C_{SP_e}, \subseteq)$ is a complete lattice.

Corollary.

Suppose SP_e is consistent and base-complete, $(GM_{SP_e}^e/\cong, \prec)$ forms a complete lattice.

When $SP_{SP_e}^e$ is complete, $GM_{SP_e}^e/\cong$ degenerates to a singleton lattice. We call SP_e^* as defined in the above proof the maximal consistent extension of SP_e.

Definition (Ext-quotient-inital model).

An ext-quotient-initial model of SP_e is a generated model for (Σ_b, Σ) that is quotient-initial and its base submodel is an initial model of SP_b. The set of all ext-quotient-initial models of SP_e is denoted by $QI_{SP_e}^e$.

Let $C_\Sigma^e \downarrow \equiv = \{c \in C_\Sigma \downarrow \equiv : c|_{\Sigma_b} = \equiv_b\}$. $\equiv \in C_\Sigma^e \downarrow \equiv$ and is the greatest element of $(C_\Sigma^e \downarrow \equiv, \subseteq)$. For an arbitrary non-empty subset N of $C_\Sigma^e \downarrow \equiv$, $c_N = \cap N$ is the greatest lower bound of N in $(C_\Sigma \downarrow \equiv, \subseteq)$. Since for any $c \in N, c|_{\Sigma_b} = \equiv_b$, we have $c_N|_{\Sigma_b} = \equiv_b$, i.e., $c_N \in C_\Sigma^e \downarrow \equiv$ and is the greatest lower bound of N in $(C_\Sigma^e \downarrow \equiv, \subseteq)$. This shows $(C_\Sigma^e \downarrow \equiv, \subseteq)$ is a complete sublattice of $(C_\Sigma \downarrow \equiv, \subseteq)$. In much the same way as we did in the proof of Fact 4.1, we can define a bijection from $QI_{SP}^e/\cong$ to $C_\Sigma^e \downarrow \equiv$ which preserves the respective orders. This gives the following

Fact 4.4.

The set of all ext-quotient-initial models of a consistent specification forms a complete lattice under homomorphism (modulo isomorphism), the initial model being the greatest element (in other words, the initial model is final in the category of ext-quotient-initial models and homomorphisms).

We have seen that, for a base-complete specification, both its extended models and ext-quotient-initial models form complete lattice under homomorphism. The only point they intersect at is the initial model, which is final among ext-quotient-initial models. This seems uninteresting. But what about the ext-quotient-initial models of its maximal consistent extension?

Theorem 4.5.

Suppose SP_e is a consistent and base-complete specification and $SP_e^* = (\Sigma, E^*)$ is its maximal consistent extension. Then $(GM_{SP_e}^e, \prec)$ can be isomorphically embedded into $(QI_{SP_e^*}^e, \prec)$.

Proof.

Let M be an extended model of SP_e. Define a binary relation $\sim_M^*$ on $|M|$ by: for any $d, d' \in |M|, d \sim_M^* d'$ iff there exist $t, t' \in T_\Sigma$ such that $d = t^M, d' = t'^M$, and t and t' are indistinguishable. From Lemma 3.1(2) and the construction of maximal consistent extension, $M/\sim_M^* \cong T_{\Sigma, E^*}$. In this way, we obtain a map $\imath : GM_{SP_e}^e \to QI_{SP_e^*}^e$ which is injective (modulo isomorphism). It is easy to verify that $\imath(M) \prec \imath(M')$ iff $M \prec M'$, i.e. $\imath$ is an embedding of $(GM_{SP_e}^e, \prec)$ into $(QI_{SP_e^*}^e, \prec)$.

We depict this fact in Fig. 1 (right).

5. Examples

We give three different specifications of finite set of natural numbers. In the following, we assume the standard specification BOOL of boolean and NAT of natural numbers (with Eq, the equality predicate).

SET0 = base BOOL, NAT
        sort set
        opns $\emptyset :\to$ set
            Insert, Delete: nat set$\to$ set
            $\in$: nat set $\to$ bool
            If_ Then_ Else: bool bool bool $\to$ bool
        eqns $n \in \emptyset = $ False
            $n \in$Insert$(m, s) = $ If Eq(n, m) Then True Else $n \in s$

$n \in \text{Delete}(m, s) = \text{If Eq}(n, m) \text{ Then False Else } n \in s$

If True Then $b1$ Else $b2 = b1$

If False Then $b1$ Else $b2 = b2$

    end

SET1 = base BOOL, NAT

    sort set

    opns $\emptyset \rightarrow$ set

        Insert, Delete: nat set $\rightarrow$ set

        $\in$: nat set $\rightarrow$ bool

        $\text{If}_{\text{set}}\_\text{Then}\_\text{Else}$: bool set set $\rightarrow$ set

        $\text{If}_{\text{bool}}\_\text{Then}\_\text{Else}$: bool bool bool$\longrightarrow$bool

    eqns $\text{Delete}(n,\ \emptyset) = \emptyset$

        $\text{Delete}(n, \text{Insert}(m, s)) = \text{If}_{\text{set}} \text{ Eq}(n, m) \text{ Then Delete}(n, s)$

                                       Else Insert $(m, \text{Delete}(n, s))$

        $n \in \emptyset = \text{False}$

        $n \in \text{Insert}(m, s) = \text{If}_{\text{bool}} \text{ Eq}(n, m) \text{ Then True Else } n \in s$

        (plus the obvious axioms for If_Then_Else)

    end

SET2 = base BOOL, NAT

    sort set

    opns $\emptyset :\rightarrow$ set

        Insert, Delete: nat set $\rightarrow$ set

        $\in$: nat set $\rightarrow$ bool

        $\text{If}_{\text{set}}\_\text{Then}\_\text{Else}$: bool set set $\rightarrow$ set

        $\text{If}_{\text{bool}}\_\text{Then}\_\text{Else}$: bool bool bool $\rightarrow$ bool

    eqns $\text{Delete}(n, \emptyset) = \emptyset$

        $\text{Delete}(n, \text{Insert}(m, s)) = \text{If}_{\text{set}} \text{ Eq}(n, m) \text{ Then Delete}(n, s)$

                                     Else Insert$(m, \text{Delete}(n, s))$

        $\text{Insert}(n, \text{Insert}(m, s)) = \text{Insert}(m, \text{Insert}(n, s))$

        $\text{Insert}(n, \text{Insert}(n, s)) = \text{Insert}(n, s)$

        $n \in \emptyset = \text{False}$

        $n \in \text{Insert}(m, s) = \text{If}_{\text{bool}} \text{ Eq}(n, m) \text{ Then True Else } n \in s$

        (plus the obvious axioms for If_Then_Else)

    end

Using induction on the structure of terms it is not difficult to check that all three specifications above are base-complete (in fact they are sufficiently complete) but only SET2 is complete. Furthermore, the maximal consistent extensions of SET0 and SET1 are equivalent to SET2.

Now consider three models *Set*, *Seq* and *SeqPair*. The interpretations for sorts *bool* and *nat* are standard. In *Set*, the carrier for the sort *set* is just finite sets of natural numbers and the function symbols are interpreted as the usual set operations. *Seq* and *SeqPair* are defined as follows:

Seq:
$|Seq|^{set}$ = the set of all finite sequences of natural numbers.
$\emptyset^{Seq}$ = the empty sequence.
$Insert^{Seq}(n, s)$ = append n to the right end of s.
$Delete^{Seq}(n, s)$ = delete all occurrences of n from s.
$n \in^{Seq} s$ = if n occurs in s then true else false.

The intepretations of *If Then Else* are as expected.

SeqPair:
$|SeqPair|^{set}$ = the set of all finite sequences of ('i', n) and ('d', n)
        where n is a natural number.
$\emptyset^{Seq}$ = the empty sequence.
$Insert^{SeqPair}(n, s)$ = append ('i', n) to the right end of s.
$Delete^{SeqPair}(n, s)$ = append ('d', n) to the right end of s.
$n \in^{SeqPair} s$ = Search in s from right to left for the first pair whose second
        component equals n. If there is such a pair and its first
        component is 'i', then the result is true, otherwise the result
        is false.

Intuitively, all three models above are correct implementations of any reasonable specifications of finite set. It is easy to see that $SeqPair \models$ SET0, $Seq \models$ SET0, SET1, $Set \models$ SET0, SET1, SET2. Also, $SeqPair, Seq, Set$ are the initial models of SET0, SET1, SET2, respectively, and Set is the final model of SET0, SET1 and SET2. Since Seq is not a model of SET2 and $SeqPair$ is not a model of SET1, it might be argued that these two specifications are too restrictive. They dictate the internal structure on the sort *set* which is supposed to be hidden from users, this seems violating the principle of data abstraction. But if we disallow mentioning any properties on invisible sorts, we would not be able to finitely specify some data types like stack. What is the solution then?

If we examine the above models more carefully, we will find that they are quotient-isomorphic. In fact, for Seq, let $s1 \sim_{Seq} s2$ iff the same natural numbers occur in sequences $s1$ and $s2$; for $SeqPair$, let $s1 \sim_{SeqPair} s2$ iff for any n, when the first pair with second component equals n in $s1$ has first component i then it must be so in $s2$, and vice versa ($\sim_{Seq}$ and $\sim_{SeqPair}$ are identities on the other sorts), we have $Seq/\sim_{Seq} \cong SeqPair/\sim_{SeqPair} \cong Set$. So, taking the maximal consistent extension of the three specifications, the sets of quotient-initial models of these extensions are the same and include all the models we are interested in.

Although SET0, SET1, SET2 are all base-complete, they differ in the new-sort, i.e. sort set. It is not difficult to see that, in that sort, SET1 is "more complete" than SET0 and SET2 is "more complete" than SET1. In fact, SET0, is the "least complete" specification and SET2 is the "most complete" one among all base-complete specifications of finite set of natural numbers. As a consequence, SET0 has most models and SET2 has least models. Indeed, GM^e_{SET0} is isomorphic to $QI^e_{SET0^*}$, GM^e_{SET2} has only one element and GM^e_{SET1} is a proper subset of $QI^e_{SET1^*}$. In other words, SET0 is free of "implementation bias" while SET2 is most heavily biased[9]. This problem disappears when the quotient-initial models of their maximal consistent extensions are taken as semantics.

6. Conclusion and Related Work

We have studied the structures of models of hierarchical specifications. We have seen that under the condition of base-completeness, both extended models and ext-quotient-initial models form complete lattices under homomorphism. Furthermore, the lattice of extended models of a hierarchical specification can be isomorphically embedded into the lattice of ext-quotient-initial models of its maximal consistent extension.

References. 3 and 15 showed the lattice structure for extended models (called "hierarchical models" there) of sufficiently-complete specifications. Since sufficient-completeness is strictly stronger than base-completeness, their results are special cases of ours.

References

Note: "LNCS" stands for "Lecture Notes in Computer Science".

1. J.A. Goguen, J.W. Thatcher and E.G. Wagner, "An initial algebra approach to the specification, correctness and implementation of abstract data types", *Current Trends in Programming Methodology. Vol. 4: Data Structuring*, R.T. Yeh ed., Prentice-Hall (1978) 80-149.
2. R.M. Burstall and J.A. Goguen, "The semantics of clear, a specification

language", *Proc. of Advanced Course on Abstract Software Specifications*, LNCS 86, pp. 292-332.

3. M. Broy, M. Wirsing and C. Pair, "A systematic study of models of abstract data types", *Theoretical Computer Science* **33** (1984) 139-174.

4. H. Ehrig and B. Mahr, "Foundations of algebraic specifications", *EATCS Monograph on Theoretical Computer Science*, Springer (1985).

5. V. Girratana, F. Gimona and U. Montanari, "Observability concepts in abstract data type specification", *Proc. 5th Intl. Symp. on Mathematical Foundation of Computer Science*, LNCS 45, pp. 576-587.

6. J.V. Guttag and J.J. Horning, "The algebraic specification of abstract data types", *Acta Informatic* **10** (1978) 25-52.

7. J.A. Goguen and J. Meseguer, "Completeness of many-sorted equational logic", *SIGPLAN Notices* **16** (1981).

8. J.A. Goguen and J. Meseguer, "Universal realization, persistent interconnection and implementation of abstract modules", *Proc. 9th Intl. colloq. on Automata, Languages and Programming*, LNCS 140 (1982) 265-281.

9. C.B. Jones, *Software Development: A Rigorous Approach*, Prentice-Hall, 1980.

10. S. Kamin, "Final data types and their specifications", *ACM Transactions on Programming Languages and Systems* **5** (1983) 97-121.

11. Lin Huimin, "A uniform framework for the specification of abstract data types", Ph.D. Thesis (in chinese), Institute of Software, Academia Sinica (1986).

12. Lin Hiumin, "Relative-completeness and algebraic specifications", *Scientia Sinica*, Seris A, Vol. XXXI No. 8 (1988) 1002-1010.

13. H. Reiche, "Behavioral equivalence — a unifying concept for initial and final specification methods", *Proc. 3rd Hungarian Computer Science Conference*, Budapest (1981) 27-39.

14. D.T. Sannella and A. Tarlecki, "On observational equivalence and algebraic specification," Report CSR-172-84, Dept. of Computer Science, Univ. of Edinburgh (1984).

15. Wirsing M. and Broy M., "Abstract data types as lattices of finitely generated models", *Proc. 9th Intl. Symp. on Mathematical Foundations of Computer Science*, LNCS 88 (1980) 673-685.

16. M. Wirsing, P. Pepper, H. Partsch, W. Dosch and M. Broy, "On hierarchies of abstract data types", *Acta Informatica* **20** (1983) 1-33.

17. M. Wang, "Final algebra semantics and data type extensions", *Journal of Computer and System Sciences* **19** (1978) 27-44.

A KNOWLEDGE BASE MANAGEMENT
SYSTEM FOR THE INTELLIGENT
MAN-MACHINE COMMUNICATION

Xie Li & Du Xing
Computer Science Department
Nanjing University, Nanjing

Abstract

KZ1/ZG is a knowledge base management system (KBMS) which cooperates with the expert system KZ1/RZ to support the intelligent man-machine
communication of operating systems. It is one component of the experimental intelligent operating system KZ1[2]. In this paper, we describe firstly the
two classes of knowledge: natural language knowledge and operating system
knowledge that are required in KZ1 and their representations. Secondly, we
present the architecture, functionality, and implementation in detail. Finally,
some conclusions of our research are given.

1. Introduction

Knowledge base management system (KBMS) is a system which provides highly efficient management of large, shared knowledge base for
knowledge directed system[1]. This highly efficient management system will
provide friendly environments for the construction, retrieval and manipu-

159

lation of large, shared knowledge base, for example, deductive reasoning, concurrent control and distribution of knowledge base over several geographic locations, etc.

Experience and practice have shown that KBMS is one of the new fields that integrate artificial intelligence (AI) and database management system (DBMS). On the one hand, in order to increase the efficiency of the system, KBMS will inherit some efficient techniques of DBMS such as data model, retrieval optimization and concurrent control, etc; on the other hand, in order to support knowledge-directed applications and increase its productivity and functionality, it will adopt some techniques of AI such as rich knowledge representation schemes, the deduction of knowledge, reasoning and explanation, etc.

Knowledge base management system KZ1/ZG is one important component of the intelligent operating system $KZ1^2$, which cooperates with the expert system KZ1/RZ to provide an intelligent man-machine communication for MS-DOS (a microcomputer OS) so that the user can interact with the system in natural language (Chinese). In other words, it provides a natural language interface for MS-DOS and the user. It has some features such as on-line execution, on-line retrieval and on-line learning, etc. In order to realize this system, one large, shared knowledge base and its management system must be provided to support the intelligent features.

Functional configuration, knowledge representation and structure schemes are key issues in KBMS researches. KZ1/ZG has following features in those aspects:

(1) knowledge base access operations are based on file system, for example, retrieval modification, knowledge reasoning and explanations;

(2) classification settlement and universal management are proposed to structure the knowledge base;

(3) the hybrid of several knowledge representation techniques such as frames, production rules and procedural approach;

(4) modular structure.

We describe the architecture of the knowledge base of KZ1/ZG in the second section of this paper, and illustrate the representation of operating system knowledge and natural language knowledge managed by KZ1/ZG in section three. In the fourth section, we describe briefly the architecture, function and implementation of KZ1/ZG. Finally we give some conclusions.

2. Architecture of the Knowledge Base

KZ1/ZG is the system used to support the intelligent man-machine communication to increase the friendliness of man-machine interaction. So the knowledge it requires can be divided into two classes: natural language knowledge (NLK) and operating system knowledge (OSK).

(i) Natural Language Knowledge (NLK)

KZ1/ZG will allow the user to describe its requests for operating system in natural language. As a result, firstly, it must own some knowledge about natural language such as the syntax and the semantics of the operation command language. Followings are several examples of natural language knowledge:

* Usually, one complete sentence must have one subject and predicate.
* Nouns can serve as subjects.
* "Observe" means to read carefully.
* "Kill" means "delete" in edit mode.

The system can use these knowledge to understand and then transform the user's requests described in natural language by means of these knowledge into an internal form.

(ii) Operating System Knowledge (OSK)

The operating system knowledge that KZ1/ZG requires is mainly the command knowledge, it includes:

* Command semantic knowledge

    This knowledge describes the functional meaning of the operating system command. For example, the command **DIR** is used to display all the directories in **MS-DOS** operating system; command **COPY** is used to backup a file. In **UNIX** system, LS is the operation to list the directories; | is a pipeline operation, which makes the output of the program before| serve as the input of the one after|

* Command syntax knowledge

    It tells the system how the command is formed. Taking the **MS-DOS** as an example, its syntax is:
    (**Commandname** [para1 [para2...]])
    The specific command COPY has the following syntax:
    (**COPY pathname** [+ **pathname**...] **pathname**)

where the pathname has the syntax:

([subdirectory\]filename)

and filename is **driverspecifier:name.extension**, and so on.
This kind of knowledge describes the syntax of the command sentences (language).

* Reference knowledge

We also take the command **COPY** as an example. Its reference
knowledge includes: the first parameter of the command specifies
the source filename, the second parameter indicates the object filename; if the first parameter is made up of several filenames which
are linked by "+", it appends these files into the object file specified
by the second parameter, etc.

* User experience knowledge

How to use commands correctly and efficiently is one of the most
important knowledge the system demands. This knowledge exists
such as the user often use **DIR** command to verify the successful
termination of the **COPY** operation, etc.

It is a major issue for a practical system to efficiently organize the
above knowledge in a knowledge base. In fact, it cost greatly to search
for a piece of knowledge in a huge, unorganized knowledge base, whereas,
a well organized knowledge base structure will give benefits to knowledge
access, retrieval and reasoning.

In KZ1/ZG, we adopt classification settlement and universal management as the organization principle of the knowledge base. Different kinds
of knowledge are stored in different knowledge bases (See Fig. 1).

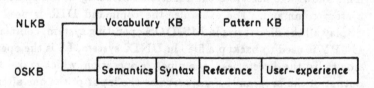

Fig. 1. The knowledge base structure of KZ1/ZG.

There are two advantages to adopt this principle: firstly, we can use
different kinds of knowledge representation approaches to make the system
more flexible; secondly, we can increase the efficiency of knowledge access
by concurrent operations of several knowledge bases.

3. Knowledge Representation
3.1. Overview

The first question we might propose is what the knowledge representation is. Generally speaking, it is a set of notations that describe the real world, it is the symbolizing process of knowledge[3]. It represents the knowledge in the form that the computer can process efficiently. A proper representation approach for domain knowledge will benefit in producing a good AI program. So knowledge representation is one of the key issues for AI programs.

Not any of the approaches can be used to represent knowledge. It must satisfy some requirements in order to utilize this knowledge. Those requirements perhaps include[4,5]:

(i) Expressive Ability: Having the ability to express the domain knowledge;

(ii) Reasoning Ability: Having the ability to operate the expressed structures. It can deduce new structures from the original knowledge;

(iii) Retrieval Ability: Having the ability to retrieve successfully the new knowledge.

In fact, knowledge representation must reflect completely the knowledge about the problem-solving domain and can be manipulated efficiently by the computer.

Generally, we divide the knowledge representation into two kinds, the first is called declarative, the second procedural. Both of the methods have their own advantages and disadvantages. The first represents most of the knowledge in the form of a group of static facts which are attached to a set of general processing programs. It separates the facts from the programs processing them; meanwhile, the new knowledge can be easily appended to the system without affecting other parts of its. The disadvantages focus on insufficient expressive power and the low efficiency of knowledge processing. Including in this approach is predicate logic, computational logic, semantic net, frames, conceptual dependency and scripts, etc. The second method, procedural method, represents the knowledge as procedures about how to use these knowledge. It has the advantages that it is easy to express the knowledge about how to solve the problems. So the knowledge can be highly efficiently utilized. But its extensibility is very poor and some knowledge is redundantly stored.

3.2. Representation of Operating System Knowledge
3.2.1. Representation of command semantic knowledge

It is recognized that frames can be used to represent the concepts of some operations to describe the semantics of the operation. So frames are adopted to represent the operating system command semantic knowledge. Figure 2 gives us an example of this knowledge which reflects the semantics of the command COPY. One Semantic Transfer Language (STL) is employed to write them. The boldfaced words are its reserved words. We do not want to go to the details, only explain some items of it:

```
( (COPY   (PRECONDITION (EXIST ⟨para1⟩
                          OBJECT ⟨para1⟩  FILE
                          CONTENT ⟨E1⟩)
          (POSTCONDITION (EXIST ⟨para2⟩
                          OBJECT ⟨para2⟩   FILE
                          CONTENT ⟨E1⟩)

          (IS-A   (FACTRULE)
          (TIME    (25))
          (WORTH   (200))
          (STATEMENT (Copy one or more files to another disk
                       and optionally gives the copy a different
                       name if you specify it in the COPY
                       command...))
          (LISP_CODE   (... Lisp code for running this command
                        in assumption environment))
          (UNDO_CODE (... Lisp code to undo the above action))
          (EXAMPLE     (... Lisp code to give examples of how to
                        use this command according to the user's
                        input parameters))
          (CAUTION      (... Warning message of this command))
          (RULE_CONCERNED (DISKCOPY BACKUP
                            RESTORE PRINT TYPE
          (FELLOW_FACT   ((DIR 2)  (TYPE 3)))
          (NEXT_FACT      (PRINT))
          (POINTER         (... address of this command
                            (knowledge corresponding in the
                            other two subKBS)))
```

Fig. 2. The semantics of the Command COPY.

* PRECONDITION and **POSTCONDITION** describe respectively the states before and after the execution of COPY command. This state change information is very useful in forming the complex commands. For example, if the user requires to type the directories on a printer, the system analyses the request and gain the goal state:

(EXIST directory PRINTER)

By using the precondition **(EXIST DISK)**, postcondition **(EXIST directory SCREEN)** of the command **DIR** and the precondition **(EXIST message SCREEN)**, postcondition **(EXIST message PRINTER)** of command Pr.Scr, the system can get the command sequence ⟨**DIR, PR.Scr**⟩ to meet the user's requirements. In the process of forming the command sequence, some inference rules are employed. We use production system to reflect these rules. For the above example, we use the rule:

{PRECONDITION1} C1 {POSTCONDITION} ,
{POSTCONDITION} C2 {POSTCONDITION2} ⟶
{PRECONDITION1} ⟨ C1, C2⟩ {POSTCONDITION2}

* TIME indicates the time for running this command **WORTH** illustrates the utilization frequency of the command. It plays an important role in reorganizing the knowledge base, we will discuss it in the next section.

* STATEMENT aspect describes the function of this command in natural language. It enables KZ1/ZG to provide the user with a readable command semantics explanation and help the user to master the command.

* RULE-CONCERNED, FELLOW-FACT, NEXT-FACE set up the relationship among the different command fact rules in semantic knowledge base. It makes it easy to transpose from one fact rule to another and catch rapidly the extract rule concerned.

* POINTER indicates the location of the rule in the other two subbase (see section 4), avoiding the searching operation when manipulating these bases. So the system performance increases.

3.2.2. Representation of command syntax knowledge

Just as the semantic knowledge frames are employed to represent command syntax knowledge. It describes the knowledge about the operating system command syntax and some concepts related to the operating system. Figure 3 shows the syntax description of the command COPY. The syntax of command COPY is defined by means of PATHNAME, which indicates a system concept using REF. Figure 4 shows that DIRECTORY and FILENAME are also the components in the definition of PATHNAME, and so on until the concepts are defined in characters and then the syntax of the command language is completely defined.

((**POINTER)   (FORMAT** (COPY var1 [+var2...] var))
                (**PARAMETER** (var1 PATHNAME NECESSARY REF)
                                (var2 PATHNAME UNNECESSARY
                                REF)
                                ...
                                (var PATHNAME UNNECESSARY
                                REF)))

Fig. 3. The syntax description of COPY.

((**PATHNAME   (IS-A** (conceptrule))
                (**DESCRIPTION** (...))
                (**FORMAT** [directory\] filename)
                (**VERIFICATION** (... Lisp code to verify if it is a
                                syntax correct pathname or not)
                (**OPERATION** (COPY DEL TYPE PRINT COMP
                RESTORE BACKUP))
                (**RELATION** (UPPER ( )) (DOWN (FILENAME)))
                (**PARAMETER** (directory DIRECTORY
                                UNNECESSARY REF)
                                (filename FILENAME NECESSARY
                                REF)

Fig. 4. The concept of Pathname.

3.2.3. Representation of reference knowledge

Reference knowledge helps the system to understand correctly the user's requests. For example, it points out that the first parameter of the command **COPY** specifies the source filename, the second parameter, the object filename and so on. Because of the complexity of the knowledge, there does not exist a uniform representation for them (or its processing efficiency is very low), we adopt the procedural approach to describe these knowledge and attach them to the corresponding fact rules. One purpose for doing so is to localize the knowledge about the specific operations of system so our system can be easily extended to serve for other operating system as the interface to the user. All the procedural knowledge is written in Lisp.

3.2.4. Representation of user experience knowledge

User experience knowledge is the key point for realizing the intelligent man-machine communication system. It is the knowledge about how the user utilizes the commands. It is updated when the user operates the system. This knowledge includes not only how to use the system but also the new knowledge deduced from the original ones. They are expressed in production rules such as this:

(VERB (type) OBJECT (file) ADJ (all)) —→ (print *.*)

this piece of knowledge is deduced when the user asks to type all files for him (or her). Another example is:

(VERB (print) OBJECT (directory) MEDIA (printer))
—→ (dir, Pr. Scr)

It is a new knowledge about the complex command which is inferred when trying to solve the user's problem "print all the directories on the printer". Because of the existence of these knowledge, the system can use them to solve the similar problems more efficiently when meeting these kind of requirements later. The main problem of this base is the maintenance such as the consistency check, etc. One approach to solving this problem is to set up models for each user; the other one is to order the knowledge in the time they are learned, then the system first use the latest knowledge. Because the memory size is limited, we adopt the FIFO strategy to "FORGET" the old knowledge.

3.3. Representation of Natural Language

According to the need for KZ1/ZG to understand natural language, we divide natural language knowledge into two classes: the first is vocabulary knowledge, which includes the meaning and usage of common words and phrases; the second is sentence pattern knowledge, which is employed to process the common sentence patterns. Generally, we assume that the concepts about the computer and the concepts about everyday life can be understood by the system. All the other concepts can be mapped into these ones (transformational semantics). For example, we use the concept DISPLAY to explain the concept SCREEN and assume that the computer can understand the concept DISPLAY.

Frame method is used to express the vocabulary knowledge in KZ1/ZG.

For example, the word **PRINT** has frame as Fig. 5.

> **(PRINT (ATTRIBUTE** verb)
> **(ALIAS** type)
> **(MEANING......)**
> **(OBJECT** message files)
> **(LOCATION** screen Disk))

Fig. 5. The vocabulary knowledge of PRINT.

It is certain that we do not store all the knowledge about the word **PRINT**, we only keep those which is necessary for the system to understand the user's requests.

Procedural method is adapted to increase the efficiency of knowledge processing. We describe all these knowledge in procedures. Three sentence patterns can be recognized by KZ1. They are:

1. declarative sentence
2. interrogative sentence
3. passive form

All the knowledge about these are described in procedures. The system will store the collocation of the sentence patterns in a pattern base for future use after it recognizes correctly the sentence pattern. For example, we have the following collocations in the base **OSKB**:

> (((explain command) 0) ((know command) 0)
> ((list file) dir) ((file-dir list) dir)
> ((file-name list) dir) ((list-file-name) dir)
> ((know file-name) dir) ...)

It upgrades the efficiency for the system to process this kind of collocations.

4. Knowledge Base Management System

4.1. Architecture

The total architecture of the knowledge base management system KZ1/ZG is shown in Fig. 6. It is divided into two parts. The first one is the direct access to the knowledge base; the second is the reasoning and explanation part which is based on the first one. The system consists of four modules: the inference module, the explanation module, the reasoning module and the access module. Its control flowchart is illustrated in Fig. 7.

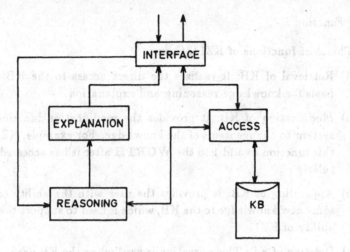

Fig. 6. The structure of KZ1/ZG.

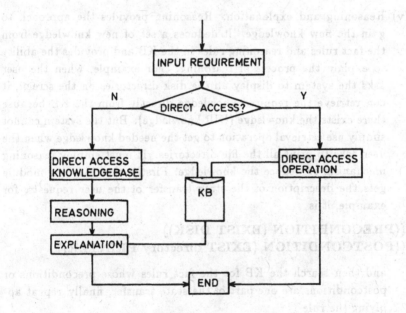

Fig. 7. The control flowchart of KZ1/ZG.

4.2. Function

The chief functions of KZ1/ZG are:

(i) Retrieval of KB: It realizes the direct access to the KB. It is the basis for knowledge reasoning and explanation.

(ii) Modification of KB: It provides the modification function for the system to change items of the knowledge. For example, KZ1 can use this function to add 1 to the **WORTH** after it has accessed this fact rule.

(iii) Appending of KB: It provides the user with the ability to append some new knowledge to the KB, which is used to support the learning ability of KZ1.

(iv) Deleting of KB: This operation is used when the KB needs reorganization. By using it, we can delete the old user experience knowledge and keep the completeness of the system functions.

(v) Reasoning and explanation: Reasoning provides the approach to gain the new knowledge. It deduces a set of new knowledge from the fact rules and reasoning rules in the KB and provides the ability to explain the process of reasoning. For example, when the user asks the system to display all the disk directories on the screen, it can retrieve the required knowledge directly from the KB because there exists the knowledge (DIR knowledge). But the system cannot simply use retrieval operation to get the needed knowledge when the user asks to print all the file directories. It must employ reasoning mechanism to deduce the knowledge. Firstly, the reasoning module gets the description of the state transfer of the user requests, for example, it is

((PRECONDITION (EXIST DISK))
((POSTCONDITION (EXIST directory PRINTER))

and then search the KB for the fact rules whose preconditions or postconditions are one part of the state transfer, finally, repeat applying the rule

{PRECONDITION1} C1 {POSTCONDITION} ,
{POSTCONDITION} C2 {POSTCONDITION2}
⟶ {PRECONDITION1} ⟨ C1, C2⟩
{POSTCONDITION2}

to get the command sequence ⟨DIR, Pr.Scr⟩. At the same time, it can explain all the process of reasoning to the user, illustrate the immediate states of the state transfer.

KZ1/ZG provides a uniform interface language for the user. All the requests proposed by the user can be described in this language. For example:

(RETRIEVE COPY **STATEMENT)**;
(DELETE DIR **USER_EXPERIENCE)**;
(MODIFY TYPE **WORTH WORTH** + 1)
(REASON precondition **(EXIST DISK)**
         postcondition **(EXIST directory PRINTER))**

, etc. The formal description of this language is illustrated in Fig. 8.

⟨**STATEMENT**⟩::= ((⟨**ACTION1**⟩ ⟨**SubKBname**⟩⟨**BODY**⟩)|
                 ((⟨**ACTION2**⟩ ⟨**SubKBname**⟩⟨**BODY**⟩)|
                 ((⟨**ACTION2**⟩ ⟨**STATE**⟩ ⟨**STATE**⟩)) ;
⟨**ACTION1**⟩::= MODIFY | APPEND | DELETE ;
⟨**ACTION2**⟩::= RETRIEVE | EXPLAIN ;
⟨**SubKBname**⟩::= SEMANTIC | SYNTAX | REFERENCE |
                USER-EXPERIENCE | NIL ;
⟨**BODY**⟩::= (⟨**ITEM**⟩⟨**CONTENT**⟩);
⟨**ITEM**⟩::= any of DOS commandname ;
⟨**CONTENT**⟩::= ⟨**Subname**⟩ ⟨**OBJECT**⟩ ;
⟨**Subname**⟩::= PRECONDITION | POSTCONDITION | TRIGGER
              TIME | ... | STATEMENT | ... | ;
⟨**OBJECT**⟩::= STRING | LISP-CODE FUNCTION DEFINITION |
             NIL ;
⟨**STATE**⟩::= STL program describing the state ;

Fig. 8. The formal description of the interface language.

4.3. Implementation

KZ1/ZG has been realized in TI-SCHEME (one dialect of Lisp) on IBM PC/AT. When designing the KB and KZ1/ZG, we try to find ways to hide the implementation details from the user and separate the functions of KZ1/ZG from the implementation of them, therefore, making the user focus on what to do rather than how to do. This has been done by means of the interface language. We define the five major functions of KZ1/ZG in Lisp functions. It is very convenient for not only the designer but also the user. Since the logic design of KZ1/ZG has been introduced in the previous sections, we now begin to illustrate the physical design of the KB.

Physically, the file system is still utilized. We store each item of knowledge in the form of files. Since the size of the KB is very large, it is impossible to reside all the knowledge in main memory. Knowledge items become the units to exchange from main memory to secondary memory and vice versa. We divide the knowledge items into two classes according to the utilization frequency (**WORTH**) and then reside the high frequency knowledge items in main memory and the low frequency in secondary memory. Each access for the system to KB will increase the **WORTH** item of the fact rule accessed. When the value of the **WORTH** increases to a certain number, it is the system itself that will dynamically reorganize the KB, keeping the high frequency knowledge items in main memory. That means the knowledge items which are often accessed will be always stored in the place where the access cost is minimal. As a result, the system efficiency increases.

So far as the system which has a large KB and limited memory resources is concerned, how to utilize the memory more efficiently to increase the performance of the total system is still open.

5. Conclusions

How to design an efficient and reliable KB and its KBMS is not only a research subject for knowledge engineering but also the key technique to make AI system practical. The design and implementation of KZ1/ZG is an experiment in this field.

The experience of KZ1/ZG has shown that the performance is still a bottleneck. We will undergo from the following aspects to improve its efficiency:

(1) adopt more efficient and more powerful knowledge representation approaches;

(2) integrate AI and DBMS to make full use of their own advantages;

(3) dig for more practical parallel algorithms to increase the speed of execution.

(4) apply the model of human memory in the field of knowledge engineering.

Acknowledgments

We are particularly grateful to Prof. Sun Zhongxiu for his advice during the project KZ1 and would like to thank Prof. Tan Yaoming and Mr. Pu Liang for their assistance. Also, we would like to thank Prof. Xu Jiafu for reading through the paper and offering useful comments.

References

1. M.L. Brodie, *Knowledge Base Management System: Discussion from the Working Group Expert Database Systems*, Benjamin/Cummings Publishing Company, Inc., 1986.
2. Xie Li et al., *An Intelligent Operating System for New Generation Computers*, to be presented.
3. Guan Jiwen et al., "On knowledge representation", *Computer Science* **1** (1987).
4. Rich, Elaine, *Artificial Intelligence*, McGraw-Hill, 1983.
5. Special issue on knowledge representation edited by Gordon McCalla et al., Computer Vol. **16**, No. 10, Oct., 1983.
6. M.L. Brodie et al., (editor), *On Knowledge Base Management System*, Springer, 1986.

FORMAL SPECIFICATION AND IMPLEMENTATION OF COMMUNICATION SYSTEM

Wu Zhimei & Ni Xizhen
Institute of Software, Academia Sinica
Beijing

Abstract

A communication system can be described with formal specification. It will be refined to an executable program through a series of transformations. A language for communication system CSL is introduced and an example is given for formal specification and refinement of communication system.

Introduction

Today the communication technology is developing rapidly and is used widely. More powerful and easy used facilities to describe and implement communication system and protocol are needed. The formal specification for a communication system or protocol is such an efficient facility. First it is oriented to problem and it is the abstract of a real system. Then after a series of transformations the formal specification can be refined into a program which is oriented to procedure, and can be executed on computer.

In the first section CSL language used for communication specification is introduced. CSL has some elements which are used to describe entity, event and behavior, they all are the components of a communication system. In second section formal specification is presented, and an example for real system is given. The third section discusses the program transformation and the last one is about the log file and rule base.

1. Kernel Language CSL

CSL is a specification language used for communication protocol and communication system. It is oriented to procedure's description. It makes the system designer and programmer easy to specify their system. In addition it also makes others easy to read and understand. There are only a few elements in CSL. Logically the description of a process can be divided into two parts, one is what variables it uses, other is what actions it takes. Corresponding CSL defines declaration part and execution part. There are two kind statements in the first part, and ten in the last one.

1.1. Declaration

* variable declaration:
  VARIABLE varname1, varname2,... varnameN

This declaration defines varname1, varname2,...varnameN as variables. They will be used in a process and keep some information for this process.

* mailbox declaration:
  MAILBOX mailboxname1, mailboxname2,... mailboxnameN

Mailbox is one kind of communication mechanism with which a series of messages can be stored. Mailbox is also used in communication process, where it puts the received message from others or sends message to other process. The mailbox uses FIFO mechanics.

1.2. Execution

* empty
  SKIP

SKIP statement does nothing.

* assignment

varname := expression

Assignment statement gives varname the value of expression.

* send message
  ! mailboxname expression

This statement sends the message in expression to mailbox. If there is some message in the mailbox, the new coming message will be in the last position of the mailbox.

* receive message
  ? mailboxname varname

This statement puts the first message in the mailbox to the variable. If there is no message in the mailbox it will put EMPTY to the variable.

* parallel statement
  // processname1, processname2,..., processnameN

This statement means these processes are executed concurrently. It finishes execution only if all of these processes stop.

* attachment statement
  + subprocessname

This statement executes a series of statement one by one, the series of statement is represented by the name of subprocessname. Subprocess means a process without any declaration.

* start timer statement
  START timername constant

This statement sets up a timer with the constant value, then starts it. There is a boolean function TIMEOUT(timername), it can show whether the timer is out or not.

* stop timer statement
  STOP timername

STOP statement stops the timer and cleans its value. After this time function TIMEOUT(timername) is false.

* if statement
  IF
      B1→ S1
      B2→ S2

......
    Bn→ Sn
ENDIF

Bi is a boolean expression, Si is a series of statement. If Bi is true, Si will be executed. This IF statement finishes after only one Si is executed.

* repeat statement
  REPEAT
        B1→ S1
        B2→ S2
        ......
        Bn→ Sn
ENDREPEAT

Bi is a boolean expression, Si is a series of statement. If one of the Bi's is true, Si will be executed. The repeat statement will be executed again until all Bi's are false. The "Bi →" can be default. It means the Bi is always true and the execution of repeat statement never ends.

2. The Formal Specification of a Communication System

There are advantages in using formal specification to describe a communication system or protocols. The formal specification is abstract of concrete system. It puts emphasis on the essential logic of the system and need not pay much attention in details. So it is short and clear. In principle formal specification can be researched mathematically, such as proving the correctness, and the equivalence of two programs. Otherwise the formal specification can be refined into an executable language through a serial transformations.

We will show an example of formal specification for communication system, this specification use CSL as language which was described in last section. Some components in CSL, such as send message statement, receive message statement, start timer statement, and stop timer statement are abstractions for primitive events in communication system.

Example: the specification of data communication on telephone network. Fig. 1 illustrated the network connection.

The data communication follows ISO standard R1745. This system can be abstracted as four parallel processes as shown in Fig. 2.

The communication between operator and station depends on the user interface, which is determined at the system requirement analysis. The

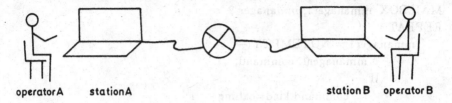

Fig. 1. Network connect

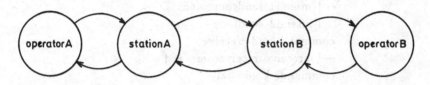

Fig. 2. Four parallel processes

communication between stations follows ISO standard. At the top level, it can be as follows:

    system
// operatorA, operatorB, stationA, stationB

The station process is complex. It can be divided into a set of process. Figure 3 shows the decomposition. Its formal specification is:

    stationA
MAILBOX mmanager1, mmanager2 mcallin, mcallout,
        mreceive, msend1, msend2, mscreen
// manager, callin, callout, send, receive, screen

The function of the manager process is to receive message from remote station and local operator. Then it delivers the message to corresponding processes. In our system there are eight operator commands, they are CALLING, SEND, RECEIVE, HALT, DISHALT, CHANGEDIREC-TION, DISCONNECT and TEST. There are four kinds of message coming from remote station, they are CALLCOMING, TEXT, ABORT and AC-KNOWLEDGE.

The specification of MANAGER process is as follows:

    manager
VARIABLE command
VARIABLE record
VARIABLE linestate

```
MAILBOX mmanager1, mmanager 2
REPEAT
    mmanager1 = NOTEMPTY →
        ? mmanager1, command;
        IF
            command.kind=calling
            → ! mcallout telephonenumber
            command. kind=send
            → ! msend1 sendcommand;
                ! msend2 sendtade
            command.kind=receive
            →! mreceive receivecommand
            command. kind=halt
            → ! mreceive haltcommand
            command.kind=dishalt
            → ! mreceive dishaltcommand
            command.kind=changedirection
            → ! msend1 disconnectioncommand
            command.kind=disconnect
            → ! msend1 stationstate
            command.kind=test
            → ! mscreen stationstate
            command.kind=ignorance
            → ! mscreen ignoranceitself
        ENDIF
    mmanager2 = NOTEMPTY →
    ? mmanager2 record;
    IF
        linestate=initial OR linestate=calling
        → ! mcallin record
        linestate=transmit OR linestate=wait
        → ! msend1 record
        linestate=receive OR linestate=pause
        → ! mreceive record
    ENDIF

ENDREPEAT
```

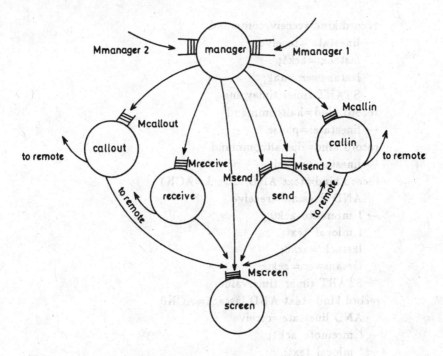

Fig. 3. Decomposition of station

The receive process deals with three local commands which refer to receiving. When receiving the RECEIVE command, it changes the line state into receive state. When getting HALT command, it changes the line state into pause state. When getting DISHALT command it changes the line state into receive state again. After getting a remote message the receive process will deliver an answer. If the message is in the right way, the answer is ACK0 or ACK1. If the message is wrong the answer is NAK. If the message is to change direction or no message in a long time. it should be displayed on the screen. This process is written as follows:

```
        receive
VARIABLE linestate
VARIABLE lastack, lastanswer
VARIABLE record
MAILBOX   mreceive, mremove, mlocal
REPEAT
    mreceive = NOTEMPTY →
        ? mreceive record
```

IF

    record.kind=receivecommand
    → linestate:=receive;
      lastack:=ack1;
      lastanswer:=nak;
      START timer timevalue
    record.kind=haltcommand
    → linestate:=pause
    record.kind=dishaltcommand
    → linestate:=receive
    record.kind=text AND lastack=ACK1
      AND linestate=receive
    → ! mremote ack0;
      ! mlocal text;
      lastack:=ack0;
      lastanswer:=ack0;
      START timer timervalue
    record.kind=text AND lastack=ACK0
      AND linestate=receive
    → ! mremote ack1;
      ! mlocal text;
      lastack:=ack1;
      lastanswer:=ack1;
      START timer timervalue
    record.kind=about AND linestate=receive
    → ! mremote nak;
      lastanswer:=nak;
      START timer timervalue
    record.kind=enq AND linestate=receive
    → ! mremote lastanswer;
      START timer timervalue
    record.kind=text OR record.kind=abort
     OR record.kind=enq AND linestate=pause
    → ! mremote halt;
      START timer timervalue
    record.kind=changedirection
    → ! mscreen changedirection;
      STOP timer
    record.kind=disconnect

```
        STOP timer
    record.kind=ignorance
    → SKIP
    TIMEOUT(timer)
    → ! mscreen  timeout
  ENDIF
ENDREPEAT
```

3. Program Transformation

Program transformation is an approach which makes a lot of relatively small alterations to a program and changes the program into destination expression step by step. The new program thus evolves from the old one, and is "better" than the old one. The idea is based on dividing a big complex problem into a series of relatively small and simple problems, and solving the problem stepwisely.

In contrast to monolithic processes, such as compilation, program transformation permits access to the program and adds the human intelligence at every step of the evolution.

The transformation approach in programming can be interpreted in two ways:

(i) Vertical Transformation: The abstract parts of a program or specification are replaced by more detail ones. In this way, some implementation decisions are incorporated into the new version. The new one has more semantics than the old one. The new one is nearer to final implementation.

(ii) Horizontal Transformation: Some parts of a program or specification are replaced in order to get a better version. The format is changed, but no semantic is added. "Better" version means nearer to the final goal.

The transformation approach in programming embodies a kind of design strategy like "divide and conquer". How to use the strategy is based on the creativity of the designer and his/her knowledge in the field of programming and in application area. For our formal specification described in Sec. 2 above, the fundamental steps of the transformation are to replace the abstract communication mechanisms, such as mailbox, send statement, receiving statement, time manage statement and parallel statement with detail realization.

The mailbox corresponds to the queue in data structure. There are queue length, front pointer and rear pointer in the data structure. Three operations are defined on the data structure, they are:

* PUTQ(queuename, message)

The message will be put on the queue where the real pointer points, at the same time change the queue length and the rear pointer.

* GETQ(queuename)

A message is taken out from the queue where the front pointer points, at the same time change the queue length and front pointer. If the queue is empty a NULL will be a message.

* CLEANQ(queuename)

The queue is set to empty.

There are two images for send message statement. IF the mailbox in the statement is at the local station, the send message statement corresponds to PUTQ operation in program. If the mailbox in the statement is at the remote station, the send message statement corresponds to a management program for line.

The receive message statement is quite similar to send message statement. If the mailbox in the statement is for the local processes, the receive message statement corresponds to GETQ operation in program. If the mailbox in the statement is for the remote station or for operator, the receive message statement corresponds a management program for the line or for the keyboard.

The start timer and stop timer statement involve a set of soft timers, which are driven by system clock.

The parallel statement corresponds to dispatch program. The parallel processes are really executed concurrently only if they are running on their own CPU. The parallel processes running on one CPU means that these processes are dispatched on some principle. In our specification the parts about communication line, keyboard or screen which are corresponding to peripheral management program have high priority, the others are dispatched in order.

Except the fundamental steps, the transformation must change the variables and the rest statements into the format of a well-defined programming language.

4. Log File and Rule Base

The transformation approach is based on the concept of the macro substitute. The rules of substitution are related to the implementation decision and the knowledge about programming. After transformation, (that means some substitute rules are practiced) a new version is produced. The log file records the history of development. The rule base is the place to put all substitution rules. Both of them are very useful in system designing and maintaining.

References

1. Stafan Jahnichen, "Language support for program developments", *Proceeding of Congress of German-China Electronics Week*, July 2nd to 8th, 1987.
2. James M. Boyle and Monagur N. Muralidaran, "Program reusability through program transformation", IEEE volume SE-10, No. 5 (September 1984) 574-588.
3. Wu Zhimei, Sun Simin, Xu Guirong and Wong Xia, "Programming for digital communication on telegraph and telephone network", Preprint of Annual Conference of Beijing Communication Society, 1983.